Keto Baking and Keto Dessert Recipes Cookbook

Low-Carb Cookies, Fat Bombs, Low-Carb Breads and Pies

Brianna Fox
Anthony Green
Copyright © 2019
All rights resered.

Table of Contents

KETO BAKING AND KETO DESSERT RECIPES COOKBOOK _____ 1
INTRODUCTION _____ 5
KETO DESSERT INGREDIENTS _____ 6
OTHER ESSENTIAL INGREDIENTS _____ 8
TIPS AND TRICKS _____ 10
TOOLS REQUIRED _____ 11
RECIPES _____ 12
COOKIES _____ 13

Samoa Bars _____ 14
Lemon Bars _____ 16
Caramel Pecan Pie Bars _____ 18
Raspberry Linzer Cookie Bars _____ 21
Almond Pecan Shortbread Cookies _____ 22
Lemon Poppyseed Cookies _____ 23
Chocolate and Pecan Cookies _____ 25
Thin Mint Macaroon Cookies _____ 27
Chocolate Chunk Cookies _____ 28
Iced Lemon Sugar Cookies _____ 29
Rasberry Almond Thumbprint Cookies _____ 31
Gingerbread Cookies _____ 33
Almond Butter Chocolate Chip Cookies _____ 35
Almond Crescent Cookies _____ 36
Maple Cream Sandwich Cookies _____ 37

FAT BOMBS — 39

- Matcha Fudge Fat Bombs — 40
- Strawberry & Cream Fat Bombs — 41
- Zesty Lemon Fat Bombs — 42
- Vanilla Strawberry Fudge Fat Bombs — 43
- Chocolate Cheesecake Kisses Fat Bombs — 44
- Lemon & Poppyseed Fat Bomb — 46
- Pina Colada Fat Bombs — 47
- Red Velvet Fat Bombs — 48
- Raspberry Cream Fat Bombs — 49
- Maple Pecan Fat Bombs — 50

BREADS AND PIES — 51

- Cranberry Bread — 52
- Chocolate Zucchini Bread — 53
- Cinnamon Almond Flour Bread — 55
- Blueberry English Muffin Bread — 57
- Pumpkin Bread — 58
- Zucchini Bread with Walnuts — 60
- 3-Ingredient Mini Paleo Pizza Bases Crusts — 61
- 15-Minute Stove Top Pizza Crust — 63
- Coconut Flour Pizza Crust — 66
- Keto Bagel — 67
- French Silk Pie — 68
- Dark Chocolate Mousse Pie — 71
- Chocolate Coconut Mounds Pie — 73
- Brownie Truffle Pie — 74
- Coconut Key Lime Pie — 76
- Sweet Ricotta Cheese Pie — 77
- No-bake Blueberry Cheesecake Pie — 79
- Chayote Squash Mock Apple Pie — 81
- Lemon Meringue Pie — 83
- Grasshopper Mousse Pie — 86

CAKES — 88

- Coconut Flour Chocolate Cupcakes — 89
- Pumpkin Pie Cupcakes — 91
- Peanut Butter Molten Lava Cakes — 92
- Texas Sheet Cake — 93

Gingerbread Cake Roll	95
Mini Cinnamon Roll Cheesecakes	99
Chocolate Peanut Butter Lava Cakes	101
Pecan Pie Cheesecake	102
Peanut Butter Mug Cakes	105
Kentucky Butter Cake	106
Chocolate Walnut Torte	108
Cinnamon Roll Coffee Cake	110
Gooey Butter Cake	112
Classic New York Keto Cheesecake	114
Italian Cream Cake	115
CONCLUSION	118

Introduction

This plan goes by many different names such as the low-carb diet, the Keto diet, and the low-carbohydrate diet & high-fat (LCHF) diet plan. However, we will keep it simple and call it the Keto diet in this cookbook!

Why go keto? The main and most visible advantage of being on keto that you will see after the first weeks (and even days) is weight loss. A low carbohydrate keto diet may also help to control hunger.

That fact may improve fat oxidative metabolism and that will help to reduce your body weight. When you are on a ketogenic diet, your body becomes efficient in burning fat as a main source of energy. When fat is used for fuel, you will feel a more consistent energy flow in your body; moreover, you won't feel the highs and lows that you would normally feel when consuming high carb food because of glucose levels spiking in your blood.

Most of these recipes are quick and easy, as we know that time is important to everybody. There are time and money saving tips inside that will help you integrate the Keto diet pretty easily into your life. You will be able to make most of these recipes ahead of time, store them for a quick snack when you need one, and some dishes are ready to be served in less than 30 minutes!

So without wasting any more time, let's get started with the main chapters of this delicious Keto Dessert Cookbook!

Keto Dessert Ingredients

There are some main ingredients that are an absolute necessity in the Keto diet to have the high-fat content that you need instead of the carbs. You will find these ingredients will be the new staple in your pantry, and here you will find out why these substitutes for your normal diet will not leave you dissatisfied. In fact, your body will thank you.

Butters

Almond butter in its purest form is simply ground roasted or raw almonds. It is a much healthier alternative to regular butter, as there are no additives like sugar and it has 3 grams of net carbohydrates per serving.

Cashew butter is a substitute for traditional butters that gives your dishes a naturally sweet flavor. It also helps your sweet treats to have a more rich and creamy dough. You may choose between 100% cashew butter, or some varieties have sunflower oil included. Note that the butter with sunflower oil will add a more oily consistency to your sweet recipes, and they will be denser.

Coconut butter can be used as a substitute in these recipes instead of butter. This is a good choice for people who have lactose intolerance or a dairy allergy.

Grass-fed butter has been shown to have higher contents of nutrients such as linoleic acid (CLA) and is loaded with beneficial fats and vitamins versus traditional butter, which generally comes from GMO-fed cows.

Hazelnut butter is another healthy alternative to regular butter, as it is high in vitamin E and manganese. You will find the more you research the Keto diet that manganese is essential in aiding in fat and carb metabolism.

Flours

Almond flour is quite popular in the Keto diet as the main substitute for the traditional wheat flours. It has a much higher fat content than wheat flour, which tends to burn recipes much quicker. You will find that many of the oven temperatures in these recipes are lower than the traditional recipes for that very reason.

Coconut flour has extremely high levels of saturated fats (which are healthy for you!), and these fats actually aid in metabolism and assist in balancing out the blood sugar levels naturally. Coconut flour has many other benefits such as being low in sugar and carbs, high in fiber, and is absolutely packed with vitamins and minerals.

Sweeteners

Monk fruit sweetener is also a popular choice; you must know that this sweetener will make your dishes sweeter versus the other choices of sweeteners. However, the people who do prefer monk fruit sweetener find that other sweeteners have a cooling effect and bad aftertaste. If you find this to be true, this will be the choice of sweeteners for you.

Natvia icing mix is a combination of stevia and erythritol sweeteners, resulting in the perfect icing that you are used to in old-fashioned recipes. But it is even better! It does not contain any artificial flavors or colors and does not cause plaque build-up on your teeth. Alternatively, you can use Swerve Icing Sugar Style in the recipes if you prefer the taste.

Sukrin Gold brown sugar substitute is also used by monk fruit lovers, as it packs the same sweet taste. This can be used as a substitute for your Keto baking needs, as it does not burn as hot as the other sweeteners and still has only 8 calories per 100 grams.

Stevia liquid drops can be used in many sweets and can be substituted particularly for the confectioner sweetener. It also contains no calories or carbs and does not alter your blood sugar levels. With over a dozen flavors to choose from, it can be the next must-have section in your pantry.

Swerve has the same amount of sweetness compared to traditional white sugars found in recipes. It measures out to be the same if converting recipes after you get deeper into the world of Keto, as you will find yourself going through your grandmother´s recipes to convert them. There are also no calories in this sweetener, so it can prevent you from feeling guilty when you are eating those Keto cookies!

Truvia is the brand name for the natural sweetener of the stevia plant. Most people who are into eating healthy have heard of stevia, or the common name of erythritol. This is a sugar alcohol that is found in melons and grapes and also has no calories.

Other Essential Ingredients

Agar-agar is based on red algae. Gelatin can be used as an alternative, but it will not have the same consistency. When you use agar-agar, you will get a firmer texture as compared to gelatin, and it has more health benefits than gelatin. It is low in carbs, sugar, and calories and suppresses the appetite, making them great treats to have when your stomach rumbles.

Fresh organic eggs are recommended versus the eggs you buy in the carton from your grocery store. This is due to them usually containing MSG, and packaging companies are not required to label this on the packaging. If you want to stay true to the Keto lifestyle, switch to the fresh organic egg option. Organic eggs are high in phosphatidylcholine, which keeps the nervous system in the brain functioning at optimal levels. They are also high in protein, antioxidants, and vitamin E so you really cannot go wrong when you make the switch.

MCT oil is an abbreviation for the fats called medium chain triglycerides. You will find high counts of these fats in coconut oil. However, MCT oil is a more potent version compared to coconut oil alone. It is an excellent aid in losing weight, as it burns more calories than it contains and it boosts your energy levels.

Mascarpone cheese comes from Italy and you will find it in the mousse recipes. You know, or will find out, that fatty cheeses are brilliant on the Keto diet, and this one does not disappoint. Because of the high-fat content, it has a more creamy consistency than cream cheese and a bonus is that the carb count is low as well!

Xanthan gum is used in particular with the cookie recipes to keep the cookies from crumbling, and it actually makes the cookies softer and tastier. It is usually an optional ingredient, but experiment with it and you may find that you cannot live without it!

Tips and Tricks

There are many tips in helping you with these recipes and others that you find along your journey into the Keto diet. Here are some basic cooking tips for this cookbook that you will find helpful for the different types of recipes.

Cookies

If you prefer to have crispy cookies while you try out these Keto diet delights, be sure to let the cookies cool completely, even if this means overnight. They will be less crumbly and you will not regret every crunch in your mouth.

If you prefer sweeter cookies, add 1/4 teaspoon stevia glycerite to any of the recipes to appease your sweet tooth.

If you find that you are not getting the fluffiness that you desire in your cookies, add 1/2 teaspoon of apple cider vinegar to the ingredients. It will alter the cookie texture, but it will give the cookies more rise.

Cakes

When you are frosting the cakes, be sure the frosting is not applied to the cake while it is still warm. This will ensure the frosting will not melt off as you are spreading it onto the cake.

Mousses

Of the recipes that are served right away without the use of the freezer or fridge, they are going to be more of the soft serve consistency. If you prefer to have a thicker mousse, simply put it in the fridge or freezer to harden it up.

Tools Required

You will have many of these cooking utensils in your kitchen already, but if you collect these tools ahead of time, it will save you time, and you will have what you need to make the Keto diet a lifestyle change for you. The items you will need that you probably already own are the absolute basics for cooking and baking. These include:

- Mixing dishes
- Electrical beater
- Stirring spoons
- Rolling pin
- Rubber scraper
- Fine mesh strainer

When you are baking sweet treats on the Keto diet, it is best to use baking paper or silicone-based pans and cooking trays because they tend to stick to the pan more so than traditional recipes. The silicone products are brilliant when it comes to baking and especially with the Keto diet, as nothing will stick to the silicone. If you choose to use the parchment paper liners, they also have the benefit of sweets not getting too wet on the bottom.

The Silpat or non-stick mat will make your life so much grander when it comes to keeping it simple with cleanup for the sweets.

And other additions are:

- Cookie scoopers
- Springform Pan
- Pastry bag

Okay, now let's jump into the recipes!

RECIPES

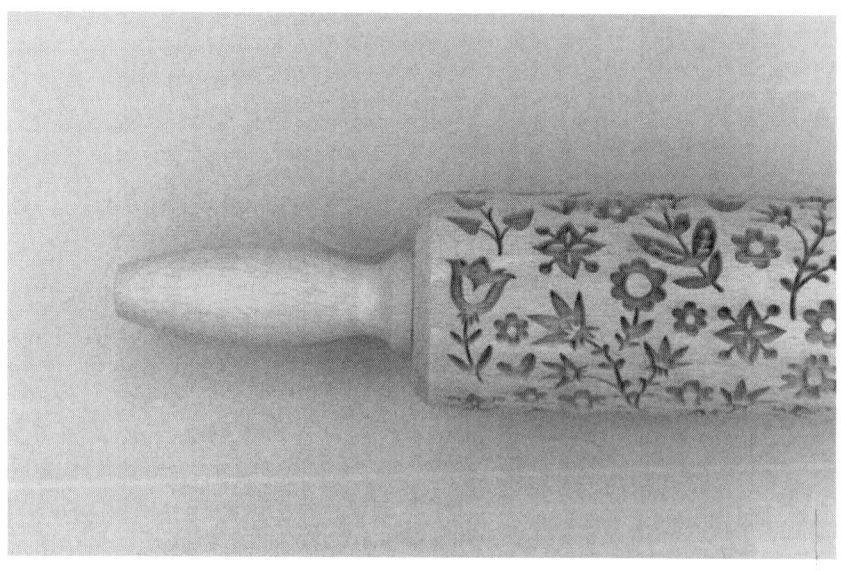

Cookies

Samoa Bars

Calories: 216/**Fat:** 19 g

Carbohydrates: 7 g/**Protein:** 3 g

Cook Time: 30 minutes
Servings: 16

Ingredients

Crust
- 1 1/4 cups almond flour (125 g)
- 1/4 cup Swerve Sweetener
- 1/4 tsp salt
- 1/4 cup butter, melted

Chocolate Filling and Drizzle
- 4 oz sugar-free dark chocolate, chopped
- 2 TBSP coconut oil or butter

Coconut Caramel Filling
- 1 1/2 cups shredded coconut
- 3 TBSP butter
- 1/4 cup Swerve Brown
- 1/4 cup Bocha Sweet or additional Swerve Brown
- 3/4 cup heavy whipping cream
- 1/2 tsp vanilla extract
- 1/4 tsp salt

Instructions

Crust

1. Preheat the oven to 325°F. In a medium bowl, whisk together the almond flour, sweetener, and salt. Stir in the melted butter until the mixture begins to come together.
2. Turn out the mixture into an 8x8 baking pan and press firmly into the bottom. Bake about 15 to 18 minutes, until just golden-brown. Remove and let cool while preparing the filling.

Chocolate Filling/Drizzle

3. In a small microwave-safe bowl, melt the chocolate and coconut oil in 30 second increments, stirring in between, until melted and smooth. Alternatively, you can melt it double boiler style over a pan of barely simmering water.
4. Spread about 2/3 of the chocolate mixture over the cooled crust.

Coconut Filling

5. In a medium skillet over medium heat, spread the coconut. Stirring frequently, toast until light golden-brown. Set aside.
6. In a large saucepan over medium heat, combine the butter and sweeteners. Cook until melted and then bring to a boil. Boil 3 to 5 minutes, until golden.
7. Remove from heat and add the cream, vanilla, and salt. The mixture will bubble vigorously—this is normal.

Stir in the toasted coconut. Spread the mixture over the chocolate-covered crust. Let cool completely (about 1 hour), then cut into squares. Gently reheat remaining chocolate mixture and drizzle over the bars.

Lemon   Bars

Calories: 190
Fat: 19 g
Carbohydrates: 2 g
Protein: 4 g
Cook Time: 20 minutes
Servings: 16

Ingredients

Crust
- 6 TBSP butter
- 2 cups superfine blanched almond flour
- 1/3 cup granulated sugar substitute (I used Swerve)
- 1 TBSP freshly-grated lemon zest

Filling
- 1/2 cup butter
- 1/2 cup granulated sugar substitute (I used Swerve)
- 1/2 cup fresh lemon juice
- 1/4 cup grated lemon zest
- 6 egg yolks
- 1/2 tsp xanthan gum
- 2 TBSP unflavored collagen powder (or 1 tsp unflavored gelatin)

Instructions

Crust
1. Preheat the oven to 350°F.
2. Melt the butter in the microwave or a small saucepan.
3. Add the almond flour, sweetener, and lemon zest, stirring until fully combined.
4. Press the dough evenly along the bottom and 1/2 inch up the sides of an 8 x 8 inch square pan. For best results line the pan with parchment paper or foil first, then you can simply lift out the completed lemon bars.
5. Bake for 10 minutes.
6. Remove and cool while you make the filling.

Filling
7. Melt the butter in a small saucepan on low heat.
8. Remove from heat and whisk in sweetener, lemon juice, and lemon zest until dissolved.
9. Whisk in the egg yolks and return to the stove over low heat.
10. Whisk continually until the curd starts to thicken.
11. Remove from the heat and strain into a small bowl.
12. Whisk in the the xanthan gum and collagen (or gelatin) until dissolved and smooth.
13. Pour the filling over the pre baked crust and spread out evenly to the edges of the pan.
14. Bake the bars at 350°F for 15 minutes.
15. Remove and cool.
16. Sprinkle with Powdered Swerve before serving, if desired.
17. Cut into sixteen 2 x 2 squares.

Caramel Pecan Pie Bars

Calories: 360
Fat: 34 g
Carbohydrates: 10 g
Protein: 4 g
Cook Time: 25 minutes
Servings: 16

Ingredients

Shortbread Crust
- 2 cups (180 g) Honeyvile almond flour
- 1 cup (65 g) shredded coconut (measured and powdered in a coffee grinder)
- 1/3 cup (25 g) whey protein powder (I like Isopure zero carb)
- 1/3 cup (45 g) Sukrin Icing Sugar (or Swerve Confectioners)
- 4 oz salted butter

Caramel Sauce
- 1/3 cup (105 g) Sukrin Fiber Syrup Gold (or VitaFiber syrup)
- 3/4 cup (177.4 g) heavy cream
- 2 oz (56.7 g) salted butter
- 1/8 tsp salt
- 1/4 cup (30 g) Sukrin Gold, powdered (or your favorite powdered sugar substitute)
- 1/8 tsp NOW Stevia Glycerite (or more of your favorite sweetener)
- 2 oz (56.7 g) salted butter
- 1 TBSP good Brandy
- 1/2 tsp vanilla extract
- 2 1/2 cups (285 g) pecans

Instructions

1. **Note:** Toasting the pecans, cooking the caramel, and preparing the crust can all be done simultaneously. This dessert can be prepared in 30 minutes.

2. Preheat oven to 350°F and toast the pecans for 8-12 minutes until they are lightly browned. Let cool completely. Chop and place into a medium bowl.

3. Spray a 9x9 inch square pan with baking spray and cut a piece of parchment long enough to fit the bottom exactly but hang over two opposite sides.

4. **Prepare the Caramel:** Measure the first 4 ingredients together in a small pot or saucepan and whisk over medium heat until combined. Bring it to a boil. Watch the heat carefully and turn it down just as the caramel mixture begins to crawl up the sides of the pot. You want the mixture boiling enough that it will get thick, but not so much that it will boil over and make a mess of the stove. Just watch it for a minute and adjust the heat up and down until you find the sweet spot. Remember, it needs to be simmering pretty quickly, but not moving up the sides of the pot. Let the mixture cook for 20 minutes. Take the low carb caramel off of the heat and whisk in the 2 ounces of salted butter, sifted powdered sweetener, stevia glycerite, Brandy, and vanilla until incorporated.

5. **Make the Shortbread Crust:** While the pecans are toasting and the caramel is cooking, measure all of the dry ingredients into a smallish mixing bowl. Mix thoroughly with a whisk. Melt the butter and add it to the dry ingredients. Stir and press the mixture with a large spoon or rubber spatula until the butter is incorporated. Squeeze a small amount in your hand to test if it will hold together nicely. If not, add 1-2 more tablespoons of melted butter. Press very firmly into the prepared pan by laying a piece of waxed paper over the crust and pressing firmly with a flat bottomed glass.

6. **Assemble and Bake:** Pour the caramel into the chopped pecans and mix together. Pour the mixture on top of the shortbread crust and gently spread it evenly over the crust. Tilt the pan a bit to distribute the caramel. Preheat the oven to 350°F and position the rack at the bottom position. Bake the Caramel Pecan Pie Squares for 25 minutes. Remove and cool completely.

7. **Serve:** Run a thin sharp knife around the inside of the pan. Pull the whole recipe of pecan bars out of the pan by pulling on the overhanging parchment. It will take a little bit of coaxing. Lay flat and cut into 16 squares. Refrigerate or serve.

Raspberry Linzer Cookie Bars

Calories: 120
Fat: 10 g
Carbohydrates: 3 g
Protein: 4 g
Cook Time: 30 minutes
Servings: 16

Ingredients

Crust
- 6 TBSP butter, melted
- 2 cups almond flour
- 1/2 cup granulated sweetener
- 1/2 tsp vanilla extract

Filling
- 1/2 cup sugar-free with fiber raspberry preserves
- 1/4 tsp xanthan gum
- 1/8 tsp almond extract

Instructions
1. Combine the melted butter, almond flour, sweetener, and vanilla extract in a medium bowl and stir well until a stiff dough forms.
2. Line an 8 x 8 baking pan with parchment paper and press 2/3 of the crust dough into the bottom.
3. In a small bowl combine the jelly, xanthan gum, and almond extract and stir well.

4. Spread the jelly mixture evenly over the crust.
5. Crumble the remaining crust mixture over the top of the jelly layer.
6. Bake in a preheated oven at 350°F for 30 minutes or until golden-brown and firm.
7. Remove from the oven and cool completely before cutting into 2 inch squares.

Almond Pecan Shortbread Cookies

Calories: 190
Fat: 20 g
Carbohydrates: 2 g
Protein: 3 g
Cook Time: 10 minutes
Servings: 20

Ingredients
- 2 cups pecans
- 1 cup almonds
- 1 cup pastured butter, melted
- 3 TBSP Swerve
- 1 tsp vanilla extract

Instructions
1. Preheat oven to 350°F.
2. In a large food processor mix almond and pecans until they turn into a coarse flour.
3. Add butter and rest of ingredients to the food processor and blend until a dough is formed.

4. Now remove the dough from the food processor and with the aid of parchment paper shape it into a roll.
5. Put in the refrigerator for 2 hrs min, until dough hardens.
6. Now slice in to 1 inch-thick rounds.
7. Place on a cookie sheet on top of parchment paper.
8. Bake at 325°F for 10 minutes.
9. Be careful not to overbake or bottom will burn!

Let cool before moving from the cookie sheet. If too crumbly, refrigerate before eating!

Lemon Poppyseed Cookies

Calories: 190
Fat: 15 g
Carbohydrates: 8 g
Protein: 5 g
Cook Time: 20 minutes
Servings: 8

Ingredients

Cookies
- 1 cup almond flour
- 1/4 cup coconut flour
- 3 TBSP poppyseeds
- 1 tsp baking powder
- 1/8 tsp salt
- 6 oz cream cheese, softened
- 1/2 cup Swerve Sweetener (granulated or confectioners)
- 1 large egg, room temperature

- Zest of one lemon
- 2 TBSP lemon juice
- 1/4 tsp liquid stevia extract

Glaze (optional)
- 1/4 cup confectioner's Swerve Sweetener
- 2 to 3 TBSP lemon juice

Instructions

Cookies
1. Preheat oven to 325°F and line a large baking sheet with parchment paper.
2. In a medium bowl, whisk together the almond flour, coconut flour, poppy seeds, baking powder, and salt.
3. In a large bowl, beat cream cheese, sweetener, egg, lemon zest, lemon juice, and stevia extract. Beat in almond flour mixture until well combined.
4. Form by hand 8 to 10 even balls. Flatten with the palm of your hand to about 1/2 inch-thick circles.
5. Bake about 20 minutes, until set and just barely brown around the edges. Remove and let cool on pan.

Glaze
6. In a small bowl, whisk together sweetener and enough lemon juice to make a thin glaze. Drizzle over cooled cookies.

Chocolate and Pecan Cookies

Calories: 66
Fat: 7 g
Carbohydrates: 1 g
Protein: 2 g
Cook Time: 20 minutes
Servings: 8

Ingredients
- 4 large eggs
- 3/4 cup virgin coconut oil, add 1/4 cup more if the dough is too dry, or add water
- 1/2 cup erythritol or other healthy low-carb sweeteners
- 15-20 drops liquid Stevia extract
- 1/2 cup raw cacao powder
- 1 cup fine coconut flour
- 1 TBSP cinnamon

Topping
- 1 bar dark 85% chocolate
- 60 halves pecan nuts

Instructions
1. Crack the eggs into a bowl and whisk with melted coconut oil. Add erythritol and stevia and mix in well. Erythritol doesn't dissolve unless heated. For best results, powder it first.
2. **Note:** To boost the flavor, you can use chocolate- or cinnamon-flavored stevia or add a tablespoon of natural sugar-free chocolate extract.
3. Add cinnamon and cocoa powder.

4. Mix in well using a whisk.
5. Add the coconut flour and process well.
6. **Note:** Sifting the coconut flour through a strainer will help you avoid hard lumps from getting into the pastry.
7. Place the dough onto a plastic foil and in the fridge to harden for at least 1 hour.
8. After 1 hour, preheat the oven to 175°C/ 350°F. Using the foil or two sheets of parchment paper, roll the dough out until it's about 1/4 inch / 1/2 cm thick.
9. Use a cookie cutter to create your shapes. I used a 2 inch / 5 cm cookie cutter.
10. Place the cookies on a baking dish lined with parchment paper, leaving little gaps between each cookie. Roll the remaining dough and repeat until all the dough is used up.
11. Place in the oven and bake for 10-12 minutes. When done, remove from the oven and let them cool down. Make sure they are completely cool before you add the chocolate topping.
12. <u>Note:</u> Coconut flour tends to burn faster than regular wheat four. Keep an eye on the cookies to prevent burning!
13. Melt the chocolate in a water bath. Using a small 1/4 tsp measuring spoon, pour the chocolate on top and press the pecan halve in. If you have any chocolate left, just spoon it on top of the pecan halves.
14. Transfer to a serving plate when the chocolate is completely solid.

Thin Mint Macaroon Cookies

Calories: 56
Fat: 5 g
Carbohydrates: 4 g
Protein: 1 g
Cook Time: 20 minutes
Servings: 24

Ingredients
- 2 cups desiccated unsweetened coconut
- 1/2 cup unsweetened almond milk
- 1 1/2 tsp peppermint extract
- 1/2 cup granulated sweetener
- 3 egg whites
- 1/4 tsp xanthan gum
- 1 oz 90% or greater cacao dark chocolate

Instructions
1. Combine the coconut, almond milk, peppermint extract, and sweetener in a medium bowl and stir well.
2. In a separate large bowl whisk the egg whites and xanthan gum together until soft peaks form.
3. Fold the egg mixture into the coconut mixture until fully combined.
4. Drop the dough mixture by scoop or tablespoon into 24 mounds onto a parchment-lined cookie sheet. Flatten into disks with your hand or a flat spatula.
5. Bake in a preheated 325°F oven for 16 minutes or until slightly firm.
6. Remove and cool.
7. Place the chocolate in a ziplock bag and melt in the microwave for 30 seconds at a time until just liquid.

Snip a tiny corner off of the bag and squeeze the chocolate out onto the cookies in a circular (or any) pattern. Cool and serve.

Chocolate Chunk Cookies

Calories: 140
Fat: 12 g
Carbohydrates: 6 g
Protein: 4 g

Cook Time: 10 minutes
Servings: 18

Ingredients
- 2 cups / 6.3 oz / 190 g blanched almond flour/meal
- ¼ tsp fine grain sea salt
- ½ tsp baking soda
- ¼ cup / 2 oz / 55 g coconut oil, melted
- 2 TBSP honey (or maple syrup)
- 1 TBSP vanilla extract
- ¾ cup / 3.5 oz / 100 g coarsely chopped +70% dark chocolate

Instructions
1. Preheat oven at 350°F (175°C), place a rack in the middle. Line a baking sheet with parchment paper and set aside.
2. In the bowl of a food processor combine almond flour, salt, and baking soda. Pulse in coconut oil, honey (or maple syrup) and vanilla extract until dough forms.
3. Remove the blade from the food processor and stir in chocolate chunks by hand. The dough will be very moist and oily—don't worry, that's how it's supposed to be.
4. Let the dough rest in the refrigerator for 30 minutes. The resting time will make the dough easier to handle.
5. Take the dough out of the fridge and scoop one level tablespoon at a time onto the prepared baking sheet.
6. With your hands, press balls of dough down gently and give them a look-alike cookie shape.
7. Bake in the oven for about 7 minutes (8 minutes for darker cookies).
8. Let cookies cool on the baking sheet (without touching) for 15 minutes, then with the help of a spatula place cookies onto a rack and let cool completely.

Iced Lemon Sugar Cookies

Calories: 96
Fat: 8 g
Carbohydrates: 4 g
Protein: 3 g

Cook Time: 15 minutes
Servings: 40

Ingredients

Sanding "Sugar"
- 2 TBSP Swerve Sweetener or other granulated erythritol or xylitol
- 1 drop yellow gel food coloring

Dough
- 1 1/2 cups almond flour
- 1/4 cup coconut flour
- 1 tsp baking powder
- 1/2 tsp xanthan gum
- 1/4 tsp salt
- 6 TBSP butter, softened
- 1/2 cup Swerve Sweetener (or other erythritol sweetener)
- 1 large egg, room temperature
- 3 TBSP fresh lemon juice
- Zest of one lemon

Glaze
- 6 TBSP powdered Swerve sweetener (or other powdered erythritol)
- 3 TBSP fresh lemon juice

Instructions

1. For the sanding "sugar," combine granulated sweetener and gel food coloring in a small bowl. Use the back of a spoon to work food coloring into sweetener granules. Set aside.

2. For the dough, whisk together almond flour, coconut flour, baking powder, xanthan gum, and salt in a medium bowl.
3. In a large bowl, beat butter with sweetener until well combined. Beat in egg, lemon juice, and lemon zest.
4. Add almond flour mixture and beat until dough comes together. Turn out dough onto a large piece of parchment paper. Pat into a rough circle and then top with another piece of parchment. Roll out to about 1/4-inch thickness. Place on a cookie sheet and chill in refrigerator for 30 minutes.
5. Preheat oven to 325°F and line another baking sheet with parchment. Cut out cookies into desired shape and lift carefully with a small, offset spatula or knife. Place cookies at least 1/2 inch apart on prepared baking sheet. Reroll your dough and cut out more cookies (if your dough gets too soft to work with, you can put it in the freezer for a bit to harden up).
6. Bake 12 to 14 minutes, or until just golden-brown and firm to the touch.
7. Let cool on pan 10 minutes, then transfer to a wire rack to cool completely.
8. For the glaze, stir powdered sweetener and lemon juice in a small bowl until smooth.
9. Spread a thin layer of glaze over each cookie and sprinkle with sanding sugar.

Rasberry Almond Thumbprint Cookies

Calories: 180

Fat: 16 g

Carbohydrates: 4 g

Protein: 4 g

Cook Time: 15 minutes

Servings: 24

Ingredients

Cookies
- 1 3/4 cup almond flour
- 1 TBSP coconut flour
- 1/2 tsp baking powder
- 1/2 cup butter, softened
- 1/2 cup confectioner's Swerve Sweetener
- 1 egg yolk
- 1 tsp almond extract
- 1/4 cup Raspberry Chia Seed Jam

Glaze
- 3 TBSP confectioner's Swerve Sweetener
- 1/4 tsp almond extract
- 1 to 2 TBSP water

Instructions

Cookies

1. Preheat oven to 325°F and line a baking sheet with parchment or a silicone liner.
2. In a medium bowl, whisk together almond flour, coconut flour, and baking powder.
3. In a large bowl, beat butter with sweetener until well combined and fluffy. Beat in egg yolk and almond extract. Beat in almond flour mixture until well incorporated.
4. Form dough into scant 1 inch balls and place two inches apart on prepared baking sheet. Press each ball down to about 1/2 inch high. Using your thumb, press an indentation into the center of each cookie.
5. Spoon about 1/2 teaspoon of jam into each and bake until just barely browning around the edges, 10 to 12 minutes. Cool on pan. The cookies will not seem set but will continue to firm up as they cool.

Glaze

6. In a small bowl, whisk together sweetener, almond extract, and water until a pourable consistency is achieved. Drizzle over cooled cookies.

Gingerbread Cookies

Calories: 130

Fat: 11 g

Carbohydrates: 4 g

Protein: 3 g

Cook Time: 12 minutes

Servings: 20

Ingredients
- 1/2 cup butter, softened
- 2 eggs
- 1 tsp vanilla extract
- 1 tsp cinnamon liquid stevia
- 1/4 cup heavy cream
- 1 TBSP molasses
- 2 cups sunflower seeds ground, or almond flour
- 1/2 cup coconut flour
- 1/4 cup Swerve or erythritol
- 1 tsp baking powder
- 1 tsp cinnamon
- 1 tsp ground ginger
- 1/4 tsp ground nutmeg
- 1/4 tsp ground cloves
- 1/4 tsp salt
- **Optional:** Chocolate chips for decoration

Instructions

1. Preheat oven to 350°F.
2. Place the first 6 ingredients into a stand mixer and blend on high until incorporated.
3. Whisk the rest of the ingredients together in a bowl.
4. Slowly pour the dry ingredients into the wet in the stand mixer.
5. Blend until combined. It will be sticky so place dough in plastic wrap and refrigerate for at least one hour.
6. Flour surface of counter with gluten-free flour and your hands with flour then pat down dough or use a rolling pin until it's 1/2 inch in thickness.
7. Use cookie cutouts for gingerbread men and place on a silpat-lined baking sheet.
8. Add chocolate chip eyes and buttons, if desired.
9. Bake for 12 minutes.
10. Allow to cool for 10 minutes before removing gently from pan.

Almond Butter Chocolate Chip Cookies

Calories: 130

Fat: 9 g

Carbohydrates: 12 g

Protein: 4 g

Cook Time: 12 minutes

Servings: 10

Ingredients
- 1 large egg
- 1 cup almond butter
- 1/2 cup light brown sugar, lightly packed
- 1 tsp baking soda
- 1 cup dark chocolate chips

Instructions
1. Set oven to 350°F
2. Crack the egg into a medium bowl and beat it lightly. Add in the almond butter, baking soda, and sugar and mix everything together well.
3. Fold in the chocolate chips.
4. Scoop the dough onto a parchment or silpat-lined baking sheet. I use a (1 3/4 inch) scoop, but you can use a tablespoon. Space the cookies well apart, and flatten them slightly with the back of a spoon.
5. Bake for 8 to 10 minutes. Don't overbake these; the cookies will look underdone, but they will firm up as they cool.
6. Let them cool for a couple of minutes on the baking sheet, then transfer them carefully to a cooling rack.

Almond Crescent Cookies

Calories: 185
Fat: 11 g
Carbohydrates: 3 g
Protein: 5 g

Cook Time: 12 minutes
Servings: 15

Ingredients
- 1 stick salted butter, softened (1/2 cup)
- Pinch of kosher salt
- 1/2 cup granulated erythritol sweetener
- 1/2 tsp vanilla extract
- 1 tsp almond extract
- 2 cups superfine almond flour
- 1/3 cup sliced almonds

Instructions
1. Beat the butter, salt, and sweetener until fluffy. Add the vanilla and almond extracts and blend well.
2. Add the almond flour and beat until just blended to a stiff dough.
3. Divide the dough into 12 balls.
4. Roll each ball into a 3 inch log.
5. Spread the sliced almonds onto a clean surface and crush slightly into smaller pieces with the heel of your hand.
6. Roll the logs in the almond pieces and then bend the two ends in and pinch slightly to create a crescent shape.

Place the almond crescents on a parchment-lined cookie sheet and bake in a preheated 350°F oven for 15 minutes. Remove and cool before serving.

Maple Cream Sandwich Cookies

Calories: 176
Fat: 17 g
Carbohydrates: 4 g
Protein: 5 g

Cook Time: 20 minutes
Servings: 24

Ingredients

Cookies
- 2 cups almond flour
- 1/3 cup Swerve Sweetener
- 1 tsp baking powder
- 1/4 tsp salt
- 1 large egg
- 2 1/2 TBSP butter, melted
- 1 tsp maple extract
- 1/8 tsp stevia extract

Filling
- 1/4 cup butter, softened
- 1 cup powdered Swerve Sweetener
- 2 TBSP cream, room temperature
- 3/4 tsp maple extract

Instructions

Cookies

1. Preheat oven to 275°F and line two baking sheets with parchment paper.
2. Whisk almond flour, sweetener, baking powder, and salt together in a large bowl. Stir in egg, butter, maple extract, and stevia extract until dough comes together.
3. Turn dough out onto a large piece of parchment paper and pat into a rough rectangle. Top with another piece of parchment.
4. Roll dough out to about 1/8 inch thickness. Using a 2-inch maple leaf cookie cutter (or whatever shape you prefer) to cut out as many shapes as possible. Dough can be re-rolled multiple times to get more cookies.
5. Place half the cookies face up and half face down on the prepared baking sheet (if your cookie cutter is slightly irregular, this allows you to match them up properly after they are baked).
6. Bake about 20 minutes, until light golden-brown and firm to the touch. Watch them carefully, they can easily get too dark.
7. Remove from oven and let cool completely.

Filling

8. Beat butter and powdered sweetener together in a medium bowl until smooth. Beat in cream and maple extract to achieve a spreadable consistency.
9. To assemble, take one cookie and spread the backside with about a teaspoon of filling. Top with another cookie, backside towards the filling.

②

Fat Bombs

Matcha Fudge Fat Bombs

Calories: 94
Fat: 9 g
Carbohydrates: 0 g
Protein: 0 g

Cook Time: 5 minutes
Servings: 24

Ingredients

- 3.5 oz cocoa butter
- 1/2 cup coconut butter
- 1/2 cup sugar-free maple syrup
- 1/3 cup heavy cream
- 3 TBSP coconut oil
- 2 scoops matcha mct powder
- 2 tsp vanilla essence

Instructions

1. Place all the ingredients in a small saucepan and place over low heat.
2. Heat until the cocoa butter has melted, stir to combine all ingredients.
3. Pour the mixture into an 8x8 inch square cake pan, lined with parchment paper.
4. Set in the fridge for 3 hours, or until firm.
5. Cut into 24 pieces and serve.

Strawberry & Cream Fat Bombs

Calories: 179
Fat: 17 g
Carbohydrates: 0.5 g
Protein: 3 g

Cook Time: 15 minutes
Servings: 10

Ingredients

- 6 oz cream cheese, softened
- 5 fl.oz double cream
- 1 oz vanilla collagen protein powder
- 3 TBSP coconut oil, plus extra 2 tsp for rolling
- 1 tsp strawberry essence

Instructions

1. Mix all ingredients with a hand mixer for 5 minutes, until well combined.
2. Set the mixture in the fridge for 1 hour.
3. When the mixture is set, rub your hands with a little coconut oil and shape the mix into 10 evenly-sized fat bombs. The coconut oil will stop the mix from sticking to your hands.
4. Store the fat bombs in an airtight container in the fridge or freezer.

Zesty Lemon Fat Bombs

Calories: 40
Fat: 4 g
Carbohydrates: 1 g
Protein: 1 g

Cook Time: 5 minutes
Servings: 10

Ingredients

- 1 oz coconut butter
- 1 oz coconut oil
- 1 oz unsalted butter
- 1 TBSP sukrin melis
- 1 lemon zest & juice

Instructions

1. Place all the ingredients into a small saucepan over low heat. Heat until just melted, then remove from the heat.
2. Pour into silicone molds.
3. Place in the fridge and chill for 1 hour, until set.
4. Enjoy!

Vanilla Strawberry Fudge Fat Bombs

Calories: 150
Fat: 16 g
Carbohydrates: 0 g
Protein: 0 g

Cook Time: 1 minutes
Servings: 32

Ingredients

Vanilla Layer
- 8 oz cream cheese, softened
- 8 oz butter, softened
- 2 tsp vanilla extract
- 3 TBSP erythritol

Strawberry Layer
- 8 oz cream cheese, softened
- 8 oz butter, softened
- 1 oz strawberry protein powder (low or no carb)

Instructions

Vanilla Layer
1. Line a baking tray with parchment paper and set aside.
2. Place the softened cream cheese, softened butter, vanilla extract, and erythritol in a bowl and mix with a hand mixer on low speed, slowly building up to medium/high speed until all ingredients are really well combined.

3. Pour the vanilla layer into the lined tray and smooth out as evenly as possible, set in the fridge for at least 30 minutes.

Strawberry Layer

4. As you did with the vanilla layer, place the softened cream cheese, butter, and strawberry protein powder in a bowl. Mix on low speed with a hand mixer and slowly increase the speed to medium/high until all ingredients are really well combined.
5. Pour the strawberry layer on top of the vanilla layer, smooth it out and set in the fridge for 1 hour.
6. Cut your fudge into bite-sized pieces and keep it cool, as it will soften very quickly in warm temperatures.

Chocolate Cheesecake Kisses Fat Bombs

Calories: 97
Fat: 9 g
Carbohydrates: 1 g
Protein: 1 g

Cook Time: 10 minutes
Servings: 24

Ingredients
- 8 oz cream cheese, softened
- 2 oz natvia icing mix
- 1 tsp vanilla essence
- 7 oz heavy cream
- 5 oz sugar-free chocolate

Instructions

1. Add the chocolate to a small heatproof bowl and place over a small saucepan of simmering water, ensuring that the bowl doesn't touch the water.
2. Melt the chocolate completely and remove from the heat. Set aside.
3. Place the softened cream cheese in a bowl, using your hand mixer, mix on medium speed until smooth.
4. Add the Natvia Icing Mix and vanilla essence and mix on low speed until combined.
5. Add the heavy cream and mix on medium speed until smooth and beginning to thicken.
6. Pour in the melted chocolate and mix on medium speed, until all ingredients are completely combined and the mixture is firm enough to pipe.
7. Add the mixture into a piping bag with a star nozzle. Pipe evenly into mini cupcake paper. We filled 24 cupcake papers, depending on your piping skills, you may get more or less.
8. Cover the kisses and set in the fridge for at least 3 hours, or overnight for best results.
9. Enjoy the kisses when set. They can be stored, covered in the fridge for up to 1 week, or frozen for up to 3 months.

Lemon & Poppyseed Fat Bomb

Calories: 60
Fat: 5 g
Carbohydrates: 1 g
Protein: 1 g

Prep Time: 10 minutes
Servings: 18

Ingredients

- 8 oz cream cheese, softened
- 3 TBSP erythritol
- 1 TBSP poppy seeds
- 1 lemon zest only
- 4 TBSP sour cream
- 2 TBSP lemon juice

Instructions

1. Place all ingredients in a bowl and using a hand mixer, mix on low speed; when ingredients are combined, mix on medium/high speed for 3 minutes.
2. Gently spoon mixture into mini cupcake cases or place into a piping bag and pipe into mini cupcakes cases. Refrigerate for at least 1 hour.
3. These cups will soften quickly in warm weather, we recommend to keep them refrigerated.

Pina Colada Fat Bombs

Calories: 23
Fat: 2 g
Carbohydrates: 0.1 g
Protein: 2 g

Prep Time: 10 minutes
Servings: 16

Ingredients

- 2 tsp pineapple essence
- 3 tsp erythritol
- 2 TBSP gelatin
- 1/2 cup boiling water
- 1/2 cup coconut cream
- 1 tsp rum extract
- 2 scoops MCT Powder (Optional)

Instructions

1. Dissolve the gelatin and erythritol in the boiling water in a heat-proof jug and add the pineapple essence.
2. Allow to cool for 5 minutes.
3. Add the coconut cream and rum extract and continue stirring for 2 minutes.
4. Pour into silicon molds and set for at least 1 hour, depending on the size of your mold.
5. Gently remove from the mold and enjoy. Store in the fridge.

Optional: If you want to get a real kick out of your fat bombs recipe try adding a scoop or two of MCT Powder, but be sure to mix it well in the hot water first (that may require a stick blender).

Red Velvet Fat Bombs

Calories: 60
Fat: 6 g
Carbohydrates: 0 g
Protein: 0 g

Cook Time: 40 minutes
Servings: 24

Ingredients

- 100 g 90% dark chocolate
- 125 g cream cheese, softened
- 100 g butter, softened
- 3 TBSP natvia
- 1 tsp vanilla extract
- 4 drops red food coloring
- 1/3 cup heavy cream, whipped

Instructions

1. Melt the chocolate in a heat-proof bowl over a small pot of simmering water. Make sure that the bowl isn't touching the water, as this will cause the chocolate to burn.
2. While the chocolate is melting, mix together the remaining ingredients with a hand mixer on medium speed for 3 minutes. Ensure the mix is fully combined.
3. With the hand mixer on low speed, slowly add the chocolate mixture to the other ingredients. Mix on medium speed for 2 minutes.
4. Add the mixture to a piping bag and pipe the fat bomb mixture onto a lined tray. Set in the fridge for 40 minutes.
5. Add the heavy cream to whipping canister and apply whipped cream to the fat bombs, as pictured.

Raspberry Cream Fat Bombs

Calories: 21
Fat: 2 g
Carbohydrates: 0.1 g
Protein: 0.4 g

Cook Time: 1 minute
Servings: 23

Ingredients

- 1 (9 g packet) raspberry sugar-free jello
- 15 g gelatin powder
- 1/2 cup water, boiling
- 1/2 cup heavy cream

Instructions

1. Dissolve gelatin and jello in boiling water.
2. Add the cream slowly while stirring and continue to stir for 1 minute. If you add the cold cream in all at once and don't thoroughly mix, the jellies will split, creating a layered affect.
3. Pour the mixture into candy molds and set in the fridge for at least 30 minutes. Enjoy!

Maple Pecan Fat Bombs

Calories: 147
Fat: 15 g
Carbohydrates: 1 g
Protein: 3 g

Cook Time: 10 minutes
Servings: 9

Ingredients

- 4 oz unsalted butter
- 2 oz pecan butter
- 1 scoop vanilla collagen powder
- 2 TBSP sugar-free maple syrup
- 9 pecan nuts

Instructions

1. Place all ingredients (except the pecans) into a small saucepan over low heat.
2. Whisk together until combined, then remove from heat. Allow to cool for 5 minutes.
3. Pour into a small heat-proof dish lined with parchment paper.
4. Sprinkle over the pecans then put in the fridge to chill.
5. Cool for 1-2 hours until set firm.
6. Cut into squares and enjoy.

Breads and Pies

Cranberry Bread

Calories: 180
Fat: 15 g
Carbohydrates: 7 g
Protein: 7 g

Cook Time: 1 hour 15 minutes
Servings: 12

Ingredients

- 2 cups almond flour
- 1/2 cup powdered erythritol or Swerve, (see Note)
- 1/2 tsp Steviva stevia powder (see Note)
- 1 1/2 tsp baking powder
- 1/2 tsp baking soda
- 1 tsp salt
- 4 TBSP unsalted butter, melted (or coconut oil)
- 1 tsp blackstrap molasses (optional [for brown sugar flavor])
- 4 large eggs at room temperature
- 1/2 cup coconut milk
- 1 bag cranberries, 12 oz

Instructions

1. Preheat oven to 350°F; grease a 9-by-5 inch loaf pan and set aside.
2. In a large bowl, whisk together flour, erythritol, stevia, baking powder, baking soda, and salt; set aside.
3. In a medium bowl, combine butter, molasses, eggs, and coconut milk.
4. Mix dry mixture into wet mixture until well combined.
5. Fold in cranberries. Pour batter into prepared pan.
6. Bake until a toothpick inserted in the center of the loaf comes clean, about 1 hour and 15 minutes.
7. Transfer pan to a wire rack; let bread cool 15 minutes before removing from pan.

Chocolate Zucchini Bread

Calories: 185

Fat: 17 g

Carbohydrates: 6 g

Protein: 5 g

Cook Time: 50 minutes

Servings: 12

Ingredients

Dry Ingredients
- 1 1/2 cup almond flour (170 g)
- 1/4 cup unsweetened cocoa powder (25 g)
- 1 1/2 tsp baking soda
- 2 tsp ground cinnamon
- 1/4 tsp sea salt
- 1/2 cup sugar-free crystal sweetener (Monk fruit or erythritol) (100 g) or coconut sugar if refined sugar-free

Wet Ingredients
- 1 cup zucchini, finely grated measure packed, discard juice/liquid if there is some - about 2 small zucchini
- 1 large egg
- 1/4 cup + 2 TBSP canned coconut cream (100 ml)
- 1/4 cup extra virgin coconut oil, melted (60ml)
- 1 tsp vanilla extract
- 1 tsp apple cider vinegar

Filling (optional)
- 1/2 cup sugar-free chocolate chips
- 1/2 cup chopped walnuts (or nuts you like)

Instructions

1. Preheat oven to 180°C (375°F). Line a baking loaf pan (9 inches x 5 inches) with parchment paper. Set aside.
2. Remove both extremity of the zucchinis, keep skin on.
3. Finely grate the zucchini using a vegetable grater. Measure the amount needed in a measurement cup. Make sure you press/pack them firmly for a precise measure and to squeeze out any liquid from the grated zucchini, I usually don't have any! If you do, discard the liquid or keep for another recipe.
4. In a large mixing bowl, stir all the dry ingredients together: almond flour, unsweetened cocoa powder, sugar-free crystal sweetener, cinnamon, sea salt, and baking soda. Set aside.
5. Add all the wet ingredients into the dry ingredients: grated zucchini, coconut oil, coconut cream, vanilla, egg, apple cider vinegar.
6. Stir to combine all the ingredients together.
7. Stir in the chopped nuts and sugar-free chocolate chips.
8. Transfer the chocolate bread batter into the prepared loaf pan.
9. Bake 50 - 55 minutes—you may want to cover the bread loaf with a piece of foil after 40 minutes to avoid the top to darken too much, up to you.
10. The bread will stay slightly moist in the middle and firm up after fully cooled down.
11. Transfer pan to a wire rack; let bread cool 15 minutes before removing from pan.

Cinnamon Almond Flour Bread

Calories: 221

Fat: 15 g

Carbohydrates: 10 g

Protein: 9 g

Cook Time: 30 minutes

Servings: 8

Ingredients

- 2 cups fine blanched almond flour (I use Bob's Red Mill)
- 2 TBSP coconut flour
- 1/2 tsp sea salt
- 1 tsp baking soda
- 1/4 cup flaxseed meal or chia meal (ground chia or flaxseed, see notes for how to make your own)
- 5 eggs and 1 egg white whisked together
- 1.5 tsp apple cider vinegar or lemon juice
- 2 TBSP maple syrup or honey
- 2–3 TBSP of clarified butter (melted) or coconut oil (divided). Vegan butter also works.
- 1 TBSP cinnamon, plus extra for topping
- **Optional:** Chia seeds to sprinkle on top before baking

Instructions

1. Preheat oven to 350°F. Line an 8×4 bread pan with parchment paper at the bottom and grease the sides.
2. In a large bowl, mix together your almond flour, coconut flour, salt, baking soda, flaxseed meal or chia meal, and 1/2 tablespoon of cinnamon.
3. In another small bowl, whisk together your eggs and egg white. Then add in your maple syrup (or honey), apple cider vinegar, and melted butter (1.5 to 2 tablespoons).
4. Mix wet ingredients into dry. Be sure to remove any clumps that might have occurred from the almond flour or coconut flour.
5. Pour batter into a your greased loaf pan.
6. Bake at 350°F for 30-35 minutes, until a toothpick inserted into center of loaf comes out clean. Mine came to around 35 minutes, but I am at altitude.
7. Remove from the oven.
8. Next, whisk together the other 1 to 2 tablespoons of melted butter (or oil) and mix it with 1/2 tablespoon of cinnamon. Brush this on top of your cinnamon almond flour bread.
9. Cool and serve, or store for later.
10. Transfer pan to a wire rack; let bread cool 15 minutes before removing from pan.

Blueberry English Muffin Bread

Calories: 156

Fat: 13 g

Carbohydrates: 4 g

Protein: 5 g

Cook Time: 45 minutes

Servings: 12

Ingredients

- 1/2 cup almond butter, cashew, or peanut butter
- 1/4 cup butter ghee or coconut oil
- 1/2 cup almond flour
- 1/2 tsp salt
- 2 tsp baking powder
- 1/2 cup almond milk, unsweetened
- 5 eggs, beaten
- 1/2 cup blueberries

Instructions

1. Preheat oven to 350°F.
2. In a microwavable bowl melt nut butter and butter together for 30 seconds, stir until combined well.
3. In a large bowl, whisk almond flour, salt, and baking powder together. Pour the nut butter mixture into the large bowl and stir to combine.

4. Whisk the almond milk and eggs together then pour into the bowl and stir well.
5. Drop in fresh blueberries or break apart frozen blueberries and gently stir into the batter.
6. Line a loaf pan with parchment paper and lightly grease the parchment paper as well.
7. Pour the batter into the loaf pan and bake 45 minutes or until a toothpick in center comes out clean.
8. Cool for about 30 minutes then remove from pan.
9. Slice and toast each slice before serving.1/2 cup chopped walnuts (or nuts you like)

Pumpkin Bread

Calories: 165

Fat: 14 g

Carbohydrates: 6 g

Protein: 5 g

Cook Time: 45 minutes

Servings: 10

Ingredients
- 1/2 cup butter, softened
- 2/3 cup erythritol sweetener, like Swerve
- 4 eggs, large
- 3/4 cup pumpkin puree, canned
- 1 tsp vanilla extract

- 1 1/2 cup almond flour
- 1/2 cup coconut flour
- 4 tsp baking powder
- 1 tsp cinnamon
- 1/2 tsp nutmeg
- 1/4 tsp ginger
- 1/8 tsp cloves
- 1/2 tsp salt

Instructions

1. Preheat the oven to 350°F. Grease a 9"x5" loaf pan, and line with parchment paper.
2. In a large mixing bowl, cream the butter and sweetener together until light and fluffy.
3. Add the eggs, one at a time, and mix well to combine.
4. Add the pumpkin puree and vanilla, and mix well to combine.
5. In a separate bowl, stir together the almond flour, coconut flour, baking powder, cinnamon, nutmeg, ginger, cloves, and salt. Break up any lumps of almond flour or coconut flour.
6. Add the dry ingredients to the wet ingredients, and stir to combine. (Optionally, add up to 1/2 cup of mix-ins, like chopped nuts or chocolate chips.)
7. Pour the batter into the prepared loaf pan. Bake for 45 - 55 minutes, or until a toothpick inserted into the center of the loaf comes out clean.
8. If the bread is browning too quickly, you can cover the pan with a piece of aluminum foil.

Zucchini Bread with Walnuts

Calories: 200
Fat: 18 g
Carbohydrates: 3 g
Protein: 5 g

Cook Time: 60 minutes
Servings: 16

Ingredients
- 3 large eggs
- ½ cup olive oil
- 1 tsp vanilla extract
- 2 1/2 cups almond flour
- 1 1/2 cups erythritol
- ½ tsp salt
- 1 1/2 tsp baking powder
- ½ tsp nutmeg
- 1 tsp ground cinnamon
- ¼ tsp ground ginger
- 1 cup grated zucchini
- ½ cup chopped walnuts

Instructions
1. Preheat oven to 350°F. Whisk together the eggs, oil, and vanilla extract. Set to the side.
2. In another bowl, mix together the almond flour, erythritol, salt, baking powder, nutmeg, cinnamon, and ginger. Set to the side.

3. Using a cheesecloth or paper towel, take the zucchini and squeeze out the excess water.
4. Then, whisk the zucchini into the bowl with the eggs.
5. Slowly add the dry ingredients into the egg mixture using a hand mixer until fully blended.
6. Lightly spray a 9x5 loaf pan, and spoon in the zucchini bread mixture.
7. Then, spoon in the chopped walnuts on top of the zucchini bread. Press walnuts into the batter using a spatula.
8. Bake for 60-70 minutes at 350°F or until the walnuts on top look browned.

3-Ingredient Mini Paleo Pizza Bases Crusts

Calories: 125

Fat: 1 g

Carbohydrates: 6 g

Protein: 8 g

Cook Time: 15 minutes

Servings: 4

Ingredients

Coconut Flour Option
- 8 large egg whites for thicker bases, use 5 whole eggs and 3 egg whites
- 1/4 cup coconut flour, sifted

- 1/2 tsp baking powder
- Spices of choice, salt, pepper, Italian spices
- Extra coconut flour to dust very lightly

Almond Flour Option
- 8 large egg whites
- 1/2 cup almond flour
- 1/2 tsp baking powder
- Spices of choice, salt, pepper, Italian spices

Pizza Sauce
- 1/2 cup Mutti tomato sauce
- 2 cloves garlic, crushed
- 1/4 tsp sea salt
- 1 tsp dried basil

Instructions

To make the pizza bases/crusts

1. In a large mixing bowl, whisk the eggs/egg whites until opaque. Sift in the coconut flour or almond flour and whisk very well until clumps are removed. Add the baking powder, mixed spices and continue to whisk until completely combined.
2. On low heat, heat up a small pan and grease lightly.
3. Once frying pan is hot, pour the batter in the pan and ensure it is fully coated. Cover the pan with a lid/tray for 3-4 minutes or until bubbles start to appear on top. Flip, cook for an extra 2 minutes and remove from pan- Keep an eye on this, as it can burn out pretty quickly.
4. Continue until all the batter is used up.
5. Allow pizza bases to cool. Once cool, use a skewer and poke holes roughly over the top, for even cooking. Dust very lightly with a dash of coconut flour.

To make the sauce
Combine all the ingredients together and let sit at room temperature for at least 30 minutes—this thickens up.

15-Minute Stove Top Pizza Crust

Calories: 120
Fat: 9 g
Carbohydrates: 5 g
Protein: 5 g

Cook Time: 5 minutes
Servings: 6

Ingredients

Keto Pizza Dough
- 96 g almond flour
- 24 g coconut flour
- 2 tsp xanthan gum
- 2 tsp baking powder
- 1/4 tsp kosher salt, depending on whether sweet or savory
- 2 tsp apple cider vinegar
- 1 egg, lightly beaten
- 5 tsp water, as needed

Topping Suggestions
- Our keto marinara sauce
- Mozzarella cheese
- Pepperoni or salami
- Fresh basil

Instructions

Keto Dough
1. Add almond flour, coconut flour, xanthan gum, baking powder, and salt to food processor. Pulse until thoroughly combined.
2. Pour in apple cider vinegar with the food processor running. Once it has distributed evenly, pour in the egg. Followed by the water, adding just enough for it to come together into a ball. The dough will be sticky to touch from the xanthan gum, but still sturdy.
3. Wrap dough in plastic wrap and knead it through the plastic for a minute or two. Think of it a bit like a stress ball. The dough should be smooth and not significantly cracked (a couple here and there are fine). In which case get it back to the food processor and add in more water 1 teaspoon at a time. Allow dough to rest for 10 minutes at room temperature (and up to 5 days in the fridge).
4. **If cooking on the stove top:** Heat up a skillet or pan over medium/high heat while your dough rests (you want the pan to be very hot!). **If using the oven:** Heat up a pizza stone, skillet, or baking tray in the oven at 350°F/180°C. The premise is that you need to blind-cook/bake the crust first on both sides without toppings, on a very hot surface.
5. Roll out dough between two sheets of parchment paper with a rolling pin. You can play with thickness here, but we like to roll it out nice and thin (roughly 12 inches in diameter) and fold over the edges (pressing down with wet fingertips).
6. Cook the pizza crust in your pre-heated skillet or pan, top-side down first, until blistered (about 2 minutes, depending on your skillet and heat). Lower heat to medium/low, flip over your pizza crust, add toppings of

choice and cover with a lid. Alternatively you can always transfer it to your oven on grill to finish off the pizza.
7. Serve right away. Alternatively, note that the dough can be kep
8. t in the fridge for about 5 days. So you can make individual mini pizzettes throughout the week.

Coconut Flour Pizza Crust

Calories: 189
Fat: 7 g
Carbohydrates: 6 g
Protein: 8 g

Cook Time: 25 minutes
Servings: 4

Ingredients
- 3/4 cup coconut flour, clumps removed
- 3 TBSP psyllium husk powder
- 1 tsp garlic powder
- 1/2 tsp salt (I love this Himalayan pink salt)
- 1 tsp apple cider vinegar
- 1/2 tsp baking soda
- 3 eggs
- 1 cup boiling water

Instructions
1. Preheat oven to 350°F.
2. Mix coconut flour with psyllium husk powder, garlic powder, and salt until fully-incorporated.
3. Add in apple cider vinegar, baking soda, and eggs. Mix together.
4. Mix boiling water in, and stir until incorporated. If the dough is too sticky, add in more coconut flour until it is the desired consistency. The dough will naturally be kind of sticky though, so you may want to use wet fingers to spread out the dough.

5. Spread dough out on a baking sheet to the desired thickness. I like mine to be pretty thin, so my dough usually covers the entire baking sheet.
6. Place in a preheated oven for 15-20 minutes, or until edges begin to brown.
7. Top with sauce, cheese and desired toppings and place back in the oven until the cheese is melted.

Keto Bagel

Calories: 638
Fat: 56 g
Carbohydrates: 16 g
Protein: 18 g

Cook Time: 25 minutes
Servings: 4

Ingredients
- 1 cup (120 g) of almond flour
- 1/4 cup (28 g) of coconut flour
- 1 TBSP (7 g) of psyllium husk powder
- 1 tsp (2 g) of baking powder
- 1 tsp (3 g) of garlic powder
- Pinch of salt
- 2 medium eggs (88 g)
- 2 tsp (10 ml) of white wine vinegar
- 2 1/2 TBSP (38 ml) of ghee, melted
- 1 TBSP (15 ml) of olive oil
- 1 tsp (5 g) of sesame seeds

Instructions

1. Preheat the oven to 320°F (160°C).
2. Combine the almond flour, coconut flour, psyllium husk powder, baking powder, garlic powder, and salt in a bowl.
3. In a separate bowl, whisk the eggs and vinegar together. Slowly drizzle in the melted ghee (which should not be piping hot) and whisk in well.
4. Add the wet mixture to the dry mixture and use a wooden spoon to combine well. Leave to sit for 2-3 minutes.
5. Divide the mixture into 4 equal-sized portions. Using your hands, shape the mixture into a round shape and place onto a tray lined with parchment paper. Use a small spoon or apple corer to make the center hole.
6. Brush the tops with olive oil and scatter over the sesame seeds. Bake in the oven for 20-25 minutes until cooked through. Allow to cool slightly before enjoying!

French Silk Pie

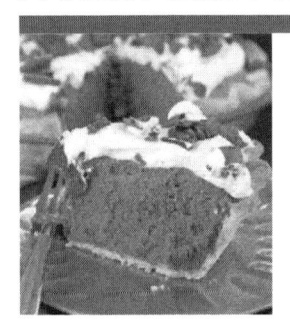

Calories: 337
Fat: 34 g
Carbohydrates: 8 g
Protein: 6 g

Cook Time: 10 minutes
Servings: 10

Ingredients

Flaky Pie Crust (or your favorite crust)

- 1 1/2 cup almond flour
- 5 TBSP butter

- 3 TBSP oat fiber
- 1 large egg white
- 1 tsp water
- 1/4 tsp salt

French Silk Pie Filling
- 6 oz (1 1/2 sticks) salted butter, very soft
- 1 1/4 cups Sukrin Melis (icing sugar) (or Swerve Confectioners)
- 1/4 cup heavy cream
- 4 oz unsweetened baking chocolate squares, melted
- 4 large pasteurized eggs, cold
- 2 tsp vanilla extract
- 1/2 tsp stevia glycerite (or more Sukrin or Swerve to taste)

Topping
- 3/4 cup heavy cream
- Chocolate shavings optional - I used 2 squares of chocolate at 86% cacao
- 2 TBSP sukrin melis (icing sugar) (or swerve)

Instructions

Crust
1. Preheat oven to 350°F. Spray a pie plate with baking spray. I use a 9 inch pyrex baking dish. (I sprinkle sesame seeds on the bottom of the pie plate so the crust doesn't stick to the bottom.)
2. Measure the almond flour, oat fiber, and salt into the bowl of a food processor. Pulse to combine. Cut the butter into chunks and pulse with the dry ingredients until the butter is the size of small peas. Mix the egg white with the 1 teaspoon of water and pour onto the dry ingredients.

Process until the dough just comes together. Refrigerate the dough for 30 minutes or up to 5 days.
3. Roll the pastry between two sheets of plastic wrap until it is the right size for your pie plate. Remove the top piece of plastic and invert the dough over the pie plate. Gently coax the dough into the bottom and the sides of the plate. Remove the plastic and shape the edge. Dock the dough with a fork.
4. Bake the crust for 10 -15 minutes, until it begins to turn a nice golden-brown. Let cool completely, then cover with plastic wrap until ready to use.

Filling
5. Finely chop the unsweetened baking chocolate and put in a microwaveable bowl. Heat on high 30 seconds at a time until almost melted. The residual heat from the bowl should take care of melting the rest.
6. Put the butter and Sukrin Melis or Swerve in a stand mixer or in a large mixing bowl. Fit the paddle attachment onto the mixer and beat the butter and sweetener on medium speed for about 2 minutes. Scrape the bowl. Add the melted chocolate and mix for 1 minute. Scrape down the bowl thoroughly. Add 1/4 cup of heavy cream, vanilla, and stevia glycerite, beating for 2 minutes more. Remove the paddle attachment, and scrape the filling back into the bowl.
7. Add the whisk attachment and turn the stand mixer back on medium speed. Add one egg at a time and let the mixer run for about 3 minutes between each addition, scraping the bowl after the third and forth additions.
8. Finish mixing with a quick burst at high speed and spread the filling into the pie shell and refrigerate. (NOTE: If the filling breaks [separates], refrigerate for 40 minutes and add 1/4 teaspoon of xanthan gum. Whip at medium speed for a few seconds to loosen the filling and then at high for

just a few seconds until it comes together. Another pinch of xanthan gum may be needed.)
9. Spoon the filling into the pie crust and smooth with a spoon or offset spatula. Refrigerate at least 6 hours or overnight, uncovered.
10. Whip the 3/4 cup of heavy cream with your favorite sweetener and top the pie. Additionally, chocolate curls can be added by running a vegetable peeler down the length of a piece of chocolate.

Serves 10 at 3 net carbs each.

Dark Chocolate Mousse Pie

Calories: 325
Fat: 29 g
Carbohydrates: 9 g
Protein: 11 g

Cook Time: 20 minutes
Servings: 10

Ingredients

Peanut Flour Crust
- 1/2 cup natural peanut butter
- 2 TBSP butter
- 2 eggs, beaten
- 1/2 tsp vanilla extract
- 1 cup peanut flour
- 1/2 tsp baking powder
- 1/4 tsp salt

- 1/4 cup low carb sugar substitute, more or less to taste

Hershey's Dark Chocolate Mousse
- 7-9 grams grass-fed gelatin, about 2 tsp or a bit more
- 1/4 cup cold water
- 1/3 cup boiling water
- 1/2 cup low carb sugar substitute, more or less to taste
- 2/3 cup Hershey's Dark Cocoa
- 2 cups cold whipping cream
- 2 tsp vanilla extract

Instructions

Crust
1. Microwave peanut butter and butter in medium bowl until melted.
2. Beat butter into peanut butter until well combined.
3. Stir in vanilla, beaten eggs, and sweetener.
4. Add the rest of the ingredients and stir until dough forms.
5. Press dough into 9 inch pie pan. Bake at 325°F for 15-20 minutes.
6. Place on rack to cool.

Mousse Filling
7. Sprinkle gelatin over cold water in small bowl; let stand 2 minutes to soften.
8. Add boiling water; stir until gelatin is completely dissolved and mixture is clear.
9. Cool slightly.
10. Combine sweetener and cocoa in large bowl; add whipping cream and vanilla.
11. Beat on medium speed of mixer, scraping bottom of bowl occasionally, until mixture is stiff.
12. Pour in gelatin mixture; beat until well blended.

Spoon into pie crust. Refrigerate at least 4 hours before serving.

Chocolate Coconut Mounds Pie

Calories: 242
Fat: 21 g
Carbohydrates: 12 g
Protein: 5 g

Cook Time: 40 minutes
Servings: 8

Ingredients

- 2 cups unsweetened coconut milk
- 4 eggs
- 1 tsp vanilla extract
- 1-1/2 tsp coconut stevia
- 2 cups unsweetened shredded coconut
- 1/2 cup unsweetened cocoa powder
- 1/4 cup coconut flour
- 1/2 tsp salt

Coconut Cream Topping

- 1 can (15 oz) coconut milk (opened, overnight in fridge)
- **Optional:** 2 ounces Lily's sugar-free coconut chocolate bar

Instructions

1. In a stand mixer with a whisk attachment blend the first 4 ingredients together.
2. Change to the paddle attachment and add the rest of the ingredients on low speed.
3. Pour mixture into a pie plate and bake for 40 minutes.
4. Allow to cool before adding coconut cream topping.

Keep refrigerated.

Brownie Truffle Pie

Calories: 370
Fat: 33 g
Carbohydrates: 6 g
Protein: 8 g

Cook Time: 30 minutes
Servings: 4

Ingredients

Crust

- 1 1/4 cup almond flour
- 3 TBSP coconut flour
- 1 TBSP granulated Swerve Sweetener
- 1/4 tsp salt
- 5 TBSP butter chilled and cut into small pieces
- 2-4 TBSP ice water

Filling

- 1/2 cup almond flour
- 6 TBSP cocoa powder
- 6 TBSP Swerve Sweetener
- 1 tsp baking powder
- 2 large eggs
- 5 TBSP water
- 1/4 cup melted butter
- 1 TBSP Sukrin Fiber Syrup (optional, but helps create a more gooey center)
- 1/2 tsp vanilla extract
- 3 TBSP sugar-free chocolate chips

Topping
- 1 cup whipping cream
- 2 TBSP confectioner's Swerve Sweetener
- 1/4 tsp vanilla extract
- 1/2 oz sugar-free dark chocolate

Instructions

Crust
1. Preheat oven to 325°F and grease a glass or ceramic pie pan.
2. In a large bowl, combine almond flour, coconut flour, sweetener, and salt. Cut in butter using a pastry cutter or two sharp knives until mixture resembles coarse crumbs. Add two tablespoons water and mix until dough comes together. Add more water only if necessary to get dough to come together.
3. Press evenly into the bottom and up the sides of prepared pie pan, crimp edges, and prick bottom all over with a fork. Bake 12 minutes.

Filling
4. In a large bowl, whisk together the almond flour, cocoa powder, sweetener, and baking powder. Stir in eggs, water, melted butter, and vanilla extract until well combined. Stir in chocolate chips.
5. Pour batter into crust and bake 30 minutes, covering with foil about halfway through. Remove and let cool 10 minutes, then refrigerate half an hour until cool.

Topping
6. Combine cream, sweetener, and vanilla extract in a large bowl. Beat until cream holds stiff peaks. Spread over cooled filling.

Shave dark chocolate over top. Chill another hour or two until completely set.

Coconut Key Lime Pie

Calories: 460
Fat: 42 g
Carbohydrates: 6 g
Protein: 11 g

Cook Time: 50 minutes
Servings: 9

Ingredients

Crust
- 2 cups raw hazelnuts
- 1 egg
- 4 TBSP chia seeds
- 4 TBSP organic butter, melted
- 1 TBSP coconut oil
- 1 TBSP Swerve

Filling
- 1.5 cup coconut cream
- 1.5 cup sour cream
- 3 large eggs
- 1 cup fresh key lime juice
- 3 TBSP Swerve
- 1 TBSP key lime zest
- ½ cup unsweetened coconut shavings

Instructions
1. Pre heat oven to 375°F.
2. In a food processor grind the hazelnuts until they turn in to a flour, then add the chia seeds, Swerve, egg, and melted butter. Mix everything together until a dough is formed.
3. Now grease a 6 by 9 inch pyrex with coconut oil.
4. Press the crust flat into the pyrex.
5. Bake for 20 min at 375°F.
6. In the meantime, prepare the filling.
7. In a large bowl mix all the filling ingredients and blend with an immersion blender until smooth and frothy.
8. Remove the crust from the oven once done.
9. Pour filling onto crust and put back in the oven at 350°F.
10. Bake for 45 minutes.
11. Remove from the oven, and let cool, then sprinkle evenly with the coconut flakes.

Then refrigerate overnight.

Sweet Ricotta Cheese Pie

Calories: 170
Fat: 12 g
Carbohydrates: 4 g
Protein: 10 g

Cook Time: 50 minutes
Servings: 8

Ingredients

- 1 1/2 cups almond flour, sifted
- 3 TBSP low carb sugar substitute (I used Swerve)
- 1/4 tsp salt
- 1/4 cup butter, melted
- 1 egg
- 1 tsp vanilla extract
- 4 eggs, beaten
- 1 tsp vanilla extract
- 15 oz ricotta cheese
- 1 TBSP coconut flour
- 3/4 cup Swerve (add more if desired; up to 1 cup)
- 2 TBSP low carb sugar substitute or 24 drops liquid stevia to help round out sweetness

Instructions

1. In deep dish pie plate, mix together almond flour, 3 tablespoons equivalent sugar substitute and 1/4 teaspoon salt.
2. Pour in butter, 1 egg and 1 teaspoon vanilla.
3. Mix until dough forms.
4. Press into pie plate. Bake at 350 degrees F for 10 minutes.
5. Set on rack to cool slightly.
6. In a large bowl mix 4 beaten eggs, 1 teaspoon vanilla, ricotta cheese, coconut flour, 1 cup equivalent sugar substitute and 2 tablespoons other sweetener.
7. Beat until smooth.
8. Pour into crust and bake at 350°F for 45 minutes or until lightly browned and firm.

No-bake Blueberry Cheesecake Pie

Calories: 325
Fat: 28 g
Carbohydrates: 7 g
Protein: 6 g

Prep Time: 40 minutes
Servings: 10

Ingredients

Crust

- 1 1/2 cups almond flour
- 1/4 cup powdered Swerve Sweetener
- 1/4 cup butter, melted

Filling

- 12 oz cream cheese, softened
- 2 TBSP sour cream or Greek yogurt, room temperature
- 2 TBSP freshly-squeezed lemon juice
- 1 tsp lemon zest
- 3/4 cup powdered Swerve Sweetener
- 1/2 cup plus 2 TBSP heavy whipping cream, divided
- 1 TBSP grassfed gelatin or 1 envelope Knox gelatin

Topping

- Blueberry syrup

Instructions

Crust

1. In a medium bowl, whisk together almond flour and powdered Sweetener. Stir in butter until well combined and clumps form.
2. Press firmly into the bottom and up the sides of a 9 inch pie pan. Refrigerate until needed.

Filling

3. In a large bowl, beat cream cheese, sour cream or yogurt, lemon juice, and lemon zest together until smooth. Beat in sweetener until well combined.
4. In a small bowl, whisk together 2 TBSP heavy cream and the gelatin. Gently warm the mixture in the microwave for about 20 to 30 seconds, and then stir until the gelatin dissolves (you can also do this in a small saucepan - do not let the cream come to a simmer). Stir into cream cheese mixture until combined.
5. In another large bowl, beat cream until it holds stiff peaks. Gently fold whipped cream into cream cheese mixture until well combined.
6. Spread filling in prepared crust, cover with plastic and refrigerate 2 to 3 hours, until set.

Blueberry Topping

Pour over the cheesecake before serving.

Chayote Squash Mock Apple Pie

Calories: 190

Fat: 16 g

Carbohydrates: 6 g

Protein: 2 g

Cook Time: 45 minutes

Servings: 16

Ingredients

Crust
- 1/2 cup butter, melted
- 1 1/2 cup almond flour
- 3/4 cup coconut flour
- 4 eggs
- 1 TBSP whole psyllium husks
- 1/2 tsp salt

Filling
- 5 medium chayote squash
- 3/4 cup low carb sugar substitute
- 1 1/2 tsp cinnamon
- 1/4 tsp ginger
- 1/8 tsp nutmeg
- 1 TBSP xanthan gum
- 1 TBSP lemon juice
- 2 tsp apple extract (optional)
- 1/3 cup butter cut in small pieces

Topping
- 1 egg
- Low carb sugar substitute

Instructions

Crust
1. Mix crust ingredients to form dough.
2. Separate into two dough balls.
3. Roll each crust ball out into pie crust.
4. Transfer one crust to 9 inch pie dish. Smooth out any cracks.
5. Reserve remaining crust for pie top.

Filling
6. Peel chayote and cut into slices.
7. Boil sliced chayote until fork tender. Drain. Return to pot.
8. Add sweetener, xanthan gum, lemon juice, and apple extract to cooked chayote squash.
9. Pour chayote mixture into prepared pie crust. Dot filling with butter.

Topping
10. Cover filling with reserved pie crust.
11. Flute edges of pie crust together and cut slits on pie top.
12. Brush egg on top crust and sprinkle with additional sweetener, if desired.
13. Bake at 375°F for 30-35 minutes (I took mine out after 30 minutes).

Lemon Meringue Pie

Calories: 218
Fat: 17 g
Carbohydrates: 7 g
Protein: 6 g

Cook Time: 50 minutes
Servings: 1

Ingredients

Pastry Crust
- 1 1/4 cup almond flour
- 2 TBSP coconut flour
- 2 TBSP arrowroot starch OR 2 TBSP oat fiber for THM
- 1 TBSP granulated Swerve Sweetener
- 1 tsp xanthan gum
- 1/4 tsp salt
- 5 TBSP butter, chilled and cut into small pieces
- 2-4 TBSP ice water

Filling
- 1 cup plus 2 TBSP water, divided
- 1 cup granulated Swerve Sweetener
- 2 tsp lemon zest
- 1/4 tsp salt
- 4 large egg yolks
- 1/3 cup lemon juice
- 3 TBSP butter
- 1/2 tsp xanthan gum
- 1 TBSP grassfed gelatin (can use 1 envelope Knox gelatin)

Meringue Topping
- 4 large egg whites at room temperature
- 1/4 tsp cream of tartar
- Pinch of salt
- 1/4 cup powdered Swerve Sweetener
- 1/4 cup granulated Swerve Sweetener
- 1/2 tsp vanilla extract

Instructions

Crust
1. Preheat oven to 325°F.
2. Combine almond flour, coconut flour, arrowroot starch, sweetener, xanthan gum, and salt in the bowl of a food processor. Pulse to combine.
3. Sprinkle surface with butter pieces and pulse until mixture resembles coarse crumbs.
4. With processor running on low, add ice water, one tablespoon at a time until dough begins to clump together.
5. Place a large piece of parchment on work surface and dust liberally with additional almond flour. Turn out dough and pat into a circle. Sprinkle with more almond flour and cover with another large piece of parchment.
6. Roll out carefully into an 11-inch circle. Remove top layer of parchment. Place a 9-inch pie pan upside down on crust and then carefully flip both over so crust is lying in the pie pan. Remove parchment. (Alternatively, you can skip rolling out the pastry and simply press the crust into the bottom and up the sides of the pan).
7. You may get some cracking and tears. Simply use small pieces of pastry from the overhang to patch them up. Crimp the edges of the crust and prick all over with a fork.
8. Bake crust 12 minutes, then remove and let cool.

Lemon Filling

9. In a medium saucepan over medium heat, combine 1 cup of the water, sweetener, lemon zest, and salt. Bring to just a boil, whisking frequently, until sweetener dissolves.
10. In a medium bowl, whisk egg yolks until smooth. Slowly add about 1/2 cup of the water to the egg yolks, whisking constantly. Then gradually whisk the egg yolks back into the pan and lower the heat to low. Cook for 1 minute more, stirring continuously.
11. Stir in lemon juice and butter and whisk until smooth. Sprinkle surface with xanthan gum and whisk vigorously to combine.
12. In a small bowl, stir together the remaining two tablespoons of water and the gelatin. Let sit 2 minutes until gelled, then stir into hot lemon mixture, whisking until well combined. Cover and set aside while making the meringue.

Meringue Topping

13. In a large bowl, beat egg whites with cream of tartar and salt until frothy. With beaters going, slowly add sweeteners and vanilla extract and continue to beat until stiff peaks form.

To Assemble

14. Preheat oven to 300°F.
15. Pour warm filling into crust. Dollop with meringue and spread right to the edges so that the meringue meets the crust. Swirl the top with the back of a spoon.
16. Bake 20 minutes or until meringue topping is golden and just barely firm to the touch. Remove and let pie cool 20 minutes, then refrigerate at least 3 hours to set.

Grasshopper Mousse Pie

Calories: 261
Fat: 25 g
Carbohydrates: 5 g
Protein: 3 g

Prep Time: 20 minutes
Servings: 12

Ingredients

No-bake Chocolate Pie Crust

- 3/4 cup unsweetened shredded coconut
- 1/4 cup unsweetened cocoa powder
- 1/2 cup sunflower seeds raw, unsalted
- 4 TBSP butter, softened
- 1/4 tsp salt
- 1/4 cup Swerve confectioners

Filling

- 1/2 cup water
- 1 tsp gelatin
- 5 oz avocado, mashed
- 8 oz cream cheese, softened
- 1 tsp peppermint extract
- 1 tsp peppermint liquid stevia
- Pinch of salt
- 1 cup heavy cream

Instructions

Crust

1. Combine all ingredients into a food processor and blend just enough to combine. Don't over blend or you will have the texture of peanut butter.
2. Taste crust to see if you need more salt or sweetness.
3. Using your fingers spread and mold crust onto bottom and sides of pie plate. Set aside.

Filling

4. Pour the water into a small saucepan and sprinkle the gelatin on top.
5. Turn on low heat, stirring constantly until gelatin is dissolved. Let cool.
6. Place the avocado, cream cheese, peppermint extract, stevia, and salt into a stand mixer and blend on high until smooth.
7. Taste and adjust sweetness if needed.
8. Pour in heavy cream in another bowl and use an electric mixer to blend on high until soft peaks form. Fold into the cream cheese mixture.
9. Gradually pour in the cooled gelatin and stir until combined.
10. Pour filling into pie crust.
11. Refrigerate at least 2 hours, loosely covered or up to 1 day.
12. When ready to serve add optional chocolate drizzle if desired.

④

Cakes

~~~~~~~~~~~

Coconut Flour Chocolate Cupcakes

Calories: 270
Fat: 22 g
Carbohydrates: 6 g
Protein: 6 g

Cook Time: 25 minutes
Servings: 12

Ingredients

Cupcakes
- 1/2 cup butter, melted
- 7 TBSP cocoa powder
- 1 tsp instant coffee granules (optional, enhances chocolate flavor)
- 7 eggs room temperature
- 1 tsp vanilla extract
- 2/3 cup coconut flour
- 2 tsp baking powder
- 2/3 cup Swerve Sweetener
- 1/2 tsp salt
- 1/2 cup unsweetened almond milk (more if your batter is too thick)

Espresso Buttercream
- 2 TBSP hot water
- 2 tsp instant espresso powder or instant coffee
- 1/2 cup whipping cream
- 6 TBSP butter, softened
- 4 oz cream cheese, softened
- 1/2 cup powdered Swerve Sweetener

Instructions

Cupcakes
1. Preheat oven to 350°F and line a muffin tin with parchment or silicone liners
2. In a large bowl, whisk together the melted butter, cocoa powder, and espresso powder.
3. Add the eggs and vanilla and beat until well combined. Then add the coconut flour, sweetener, baking powder and salt and beat until smooth.
4. Beat in the almond milk. If that batter is still very thick, beat in more almond milk 1 tablespoon at a time until it thins out a bit (batter will still be thick, but should be of scoopable consistency; it will not be pourable).
5. Divide batter among prepared muffin tins and bake in center of oven for 20 to 25 minutes. Cupcakes are done when the top is set and a tester inserted into the middle comes out clean. Cool in pan for 5-10 minutes and then transfer to a wire rack to cool completely.

Buttercream
6. In a small bowl, stir together hot water and espresso until coffee dissolves. Set aside.
7. With an electric mixer, whip cream until it forms stiff peaks. Set aside.
8. In a medium bowl, beat butter, cream cheese, and sweetener together until creamy. Add coffee mixture and beat until combined. With a rubber spatula, fold in whipped cream carefully until well combined.
9. Spread frosting on cooled cupcakes with a knife or offset spatula, or pipe on with a decorating bag.

Pumpkin Pie Cupcakes

Calories: 70
Fat: 4 g
Carbohydrates: 5 g
Protein: 2 g

Cook Time: 30 minutes
Servings: 6

Ingredients
- 3 TBSP coconut flour
- 1 tsp pumpkin pie spice
- 1/4 tsp baking powder
- 1/4 tsp baking soda
- Pinch of salt
- 3/4 cup pumpkin puree
- 1/3 cup Swerve Brown or Swerve Granular
- 1/4 cup heavy whipping cream
- 1 large egg
- 1/2 tsp vanilla

Instructions

1. Preheat oven to 350°F and line 6 muffin cups with silicone or parchment liners.
2. In a small bowl, whisk together the coconut flour, pumpkin pie spice, baking powder, baking soda, and salt.
3. In a large bowl, whisk pumpkin puree, sweetener, cream, egg, and vanilla until well combined. Whisk in dry ingredients. If your batter seems very thin, whisk in an additional tbsp of coconut flour.
4. Divide among prepared muffin cups and bake 25 to 30 minutes, until just puffed and barely set. Remove from oven and let cool in pan (they will sink...that's okay, all the better for plopping your whipped cream on top!).
5. Refrigerate for at least one hour before serving. Dollop whipped cream generously on top.

Peanut Butter Molten Lava Cakes

Calories: 390
Fat: 35 g
Carbohydrates: 6 g
Protein: 10 g

Cook Time: 20 minutes
Servings: 4

Ingredients
- 1/4 cup butter
- 1/4 cup peanut butter
- 2 TBSP coconut oil
- 6 TBSP powdered Swerve Sweetener
- 2 large eggs
- 2 large egg yolks
- 1/2 tsp vanilla extract
- 6 TBSP almond flour
- Low carb chocolate sauce

Instructions
1. Preheat oven to 350°F and grease 4 small (about 1/2 cup capacity each) ramekins very well. I used both butter AND coconut oil spray.
2. In a medium-sized microwave safe bowl, combine butter, peanut butter, and coconut oil. Cook on high in 30 second increments until melted. Stir together until smooth.
3. Whisk in powdered sweetener until smooth. Whisk in eggs, egg yolks, and vanilla extract. Then whisk in almond flour until smooth.
4. Divide batter among prepared ramekins and bake 12 to 15 minutes, until sides are set but the center still jiggles a bit. Remove and let cool a few minutes.

5. Run a sharp knife around the inside of the ramekin to loosen the cakes. Cover each with an upside-down plate and flip over to turn the cake out onto the plate (you may need to give it one good shake, holding the plate and ramekin together tightly).
6. Drizzle with low carb chocolate sauce and serve immediately.

Texas Sheet Cake

Calories: 230

Fat: 20 g

Carbohydrates: 6 g

Protein: 6 g

Cook Time: 30 minutes

Servings: 20

Ingredients

Cake
- 2 cups almond flour
- 3/4 cup Swerve Sweetener
- 1/3 cup coconut flour
- 1/3 cup unflavoured whey protein powder
- 1 TBSP baking powder
- 1/2 tsp salt
- 1/2 cup butter
- 1/2 cup water
- 1/4 cup cocoa powder

- 3 large eggs
- 1 tsp vanilla extract
- 1/4 cup heavy cream
- 1/4 cup water

Frosting
- 1/2 cup butter
- 1/4 cup cocoa powder
- 1/4 cup cream
- 1/4 cup water
- 1 tsp vanilla extract
- 1 1/2 cups powdered Swerve Sweetener
- 1/4 tsp xanthan gum
- 3/4 cup chopped pecans

Instructions

Cake
1. Preheat oven to 325°F and grease a 10x15 inch rimmed sheet pan very well.
2. In a large bowl, whisk together the almond flour, sweetener, coconut flour, protein powder, baking powder, and salt. Break up any clumps with the back of a fork.
3. In a medium saucepan over medium heat, combine the butter, water, and cocoa powder, stirring until melted. Bring to a boil and then remove from heat. Add to the bowl.
4. Add eggs, vanilla extract, cream and water and stir until well combined. Spread in prepared baking pan.
5. Bake 15 to 20 minutes, until cake is set and a tester inserted in the center comes out clean.

Frosting

6. In another medium saucepan, combine butter, cocoa powder, cream, and water. Bring to a simmer, stirring until smooth. Stir in vanilla extract. Add powdered sweetener 1/2 a cup at a time, whisking vigorously to dissolve any clumps. Whisk in xanthan gum.
7. Pour over warm cake and sprinkle with pecans. Let cool until frosting is set, about 1 hour.

Gingerbread Cake Roll

Calories: 206
Fat: 18 g
Carbohydrates: 4 g
Protein: 6 g
Cook Time: 15 minutes
Servings: 12

Ingredients

Cake
- 1 cup almond flour
- 1/4 cup powdered Swerve Sweetener
- 2 TBSP cocoa powder
- 1 TBSP grassfed gelatin
- 2 tsp ground ginger
- 1 tsp ground cinnamon
- 1/4 tsp ground cloves
- 4 large eggs room temperature, separated
- 1/4 cup granulated Swerve Sweetener, divided
- 1 tsp vanilla extract
- 1/4 tsp salt, divided

- 1/4 tsp cream of tartar

Vanilla Cream Filling
- 2 oz cream cheese, softened
- 1 1/2 cups whipping cream, divided
- 1/4 cup powdered Swerve Sweetener
- 1/2 tsp vanilla extract

Instructions

Cake

1. Preheat oven to 350°F and line an 11x17 inch rimmed baking sheet with parchment paper. Grease the parchment paper and pan sides very well.
2. In a medium bowl, whisk together the almond flour, powdered sweetener, cocoa powder, gelatin, ginger, cinnamon, and cloves.
3. In another medium bowl, beat the egg yolks with 2 tablespoons of the granulated sweetener until lighter yellow and thickened. Beat in the vanilla extract
4. Using clean beaters and a large clean bowl, beat the egg whites with the salt and cream of tartar until frothy. Beat in the remaining two tablespoons sweetener until stiff peaks form.
5. Gently fold the egg yolk mixture into the whites. Then gently fold in the almond flour mixture, taking care not to deflate them, until no streaks remain.

6. Spread the batter evenly into the prepared baking pan and bake 10 to 12 minutes, until the top springs back when touched.
7. Remove from the oven and let let cool a few minutes, then run a knife around the edges to loosen. Cover with another large piece of parchment paper and then a kitchen towel. Place another large baking sheet overtop and flip over.
8. Gently peel the parchment from what is now the top of the cake. While still warm, gently roll up inside the kitchen towel, starting from one of the shorter ends. Don't roll too tightly or it will crack. Let cool while preparing the filling.

Vanilla Cream Filling

9. In a small bowl, beat the cream cheese with 1/4 cup whipping cream until smooth.
10. In a large bowl, beat the remaining whipping cream with the sweetener and vanilla extract until it holds soft peaks. Then add the cream cheese mixture and continue to beat until stiff peaks form. Do not over-beat. Remove 1/2 cup and set aside for decorating.
11. Gently and carefully unroll the cake. Do not try to lay it completely flat, let it curl up on the ends. Spread with the remaining filling to within 1/2 inch of the edges. Gently roll back up without the kitchen towel. Place seam side-down on a serving platter.

12. Sprinkle with some more powdered sweetener, if desired. Pipe remaining vanilla cream mixture in stars or other shapes down the center of the top of the cake.
13. Refrigerate 1 hour before slicing. Store in the refrigerator.

Mini Cinnamon Roll Cheesecakes

Calories: 240

Fat: 20 g

Carbohydrates: 5 g

Protein: 5 g

Cook Time: 30 minutes

Servings: 6

Ingredients

Crust
- 1/2 cup almond flour
- 2 TBSP Swerve Sweetener
- 1/2 tsp cinnamon
- 2 TBSP melted butter

Cheesecake Filling
- 6 oz cream cheese, softened
- 5 TBSP Swerve Sweetener, divided
- 1/4 cup sour cream
- 1/2 tsp vanilla extract
- 1 large egg
- 2 tsp cinnamon

Frosting
- 1 TBSP butter, softened
- 3 TBSP confectioners Swerve Sweetener
- 1/4 tsp vanilla extract
- 2 tsp heavy cream

Instructions

Crust

1. Preheat the oven to 325°F and line a muffin pan with 6 parchment or silicone liners.
2. In a medium bowl, whisk together the almond flour, sweetener and cinnamon. Stir in the melted butter until the mixture begins to clump together.
3. Divide among the prepared muffin cups and press firmly into the bottom. Bake 7 minutes, then remove and let cool while preparing the filling.

Cheesecake Filling

4. Reduce oven temperature to 300°F. In a large bowl, beat the cream cheese and 3 tablespoons of the sweetener together until smooth. Beat in the sour cream, vanilla and egg until well combined.
5. In a small bowl, whisk together the remaining 2 tablespoons sweetener and the cinnamon.
6. Dollop about 3/4 tablespoon of the cream cheese mixture into each of the muffin cups and sprinkle with a little of the cinnamon mixture. Repeat 2 more times. If you have any leftover cinnamon "sugar," reserve to sprinkle on after the cheesecakes are baked.
7. Bake 15 to 17 minutes, until mostly set but centres jiggle slightly. Turn off the oven and let them remain inside for 5 more minutes, then remove and let cool 30 minutes. Refrigerate at least 2 hours until set.

Frosting

8. In a medium bowl, beat butter with powdered sweetener until well combined. Beat in vanilla extract and heavy cream.
9. Transfer to a small ziplock bag and snip the corner. Drizzle decoratively over the chilled cheesecakes.

Chocolate Peanut Butter Lava Cakes

Calories: 345
Fat: 30 g
Carbohydrates: 7 g
Protein: 8 g

Cook Time: 12 minutes
Servings: 3

Ingredients

- 1/4 cup butter
- 1 oz unsweetened chocolate chopped
- 3 TBSP Swerve Sweetener
- 1 large egg
- 1 large egg yolk
- 3 TBSP almond flour
- 1/4 tsp vanilla extract
- Pinch of salt
- 2 TBSP peanut butter

Instructions

1. Preheat oven to 375°F and grease 3 small ramekins. Dust the ramekins with cocoa powder and shake out the excess.
2. In a microwave safe bowl, melt butter and chocolate together, whisking until smooth. Alternatively, you can melt it carefully over low heat.
3. Add the sweetener and whisk until combined. Then add the egg and egg yolk and whisk until smooth.
4. Whisk in the almond flour, vanilla extract, and salt until well combined.
5. Divide about 2/3 of the batter between the three ramekins, making sure to cover the bottom.
6. Divide peanut butter between the ramekins, placing in center of the batter. Cover with remaining batter. Bake 10 to 12 minutes, or until the edges of the cakes are set but the center still jiggles slightly. Remove and let cool 5 to 10 minutes. Then run a sharp knife around the edges and flip out onto plates.

Pecan Pie Cheesecake

Calories: 340
Fat: 30 g
Carbohydrates: 5 g
Protein: 6 g

Cook Time: 35 minutes
Servings: 10

Ingredients

Crust
- 3/4 cup almond flour
- 2 TBSP powdered Swerve Sweetener
- Pinch of salt
- 2 TBSP melted butter

Pecan Pie Filling
- 1/4 cup butter
- 1/3 cup powdered Swerve Sweetener
- 1 tsp Yacon syrup or molasses optional, for color and flavor
- 1 tsp caramel extract or vanilla extract
- 2 TBSP heavy whipping cream
- 1 large egg
- 1/4 tsp salt
- 1/2 cup chopped pecans

Cheesecake Filling
- 12 oz cream cheese, softened
- 5 TBSP powdered Swerve Sweetener
- 1 large egg
- 1/4 cup heavy whipping cream

- 1/2 tsp vanilla extract

Topping
- 2 TBSP butter
- 2 1/2 tbsp powdered Swerve Sweetener
- 1/2 tsp Yacon syrup or molasses
- 1/2 tsp caramel extract or vanilla extract
- 1 TBSP heavy whipping cream
- Whole toasted pecans for garnish

Instructions

Crust

1. In a medium bowl, whisk together the almond flour, sweetener, and salt. Stir in the melted butter until the mixture begins to clump together.
2. Press into the bottom and partway up the sides of a 7-inch springform pan. Place in the freezer while making the pecan pie filling.

Pecan Pie Filling

3. In a small saucepan over low heat, melt the butter. Add the sweetener and Yacon syrup and whisk until combined, then stir in the extract and heavy whipping cream.
4. Add the egg and continue to cook over low heat until the mixture thickens (this should only take a minute or so). Immediately remove from heat and stir in the pecans and salt.
5. Spread mixture over the bottom of the crust.

Cheesecake Filling

6. Beat the cream cheese until smooth, then beat in the sweetener. Beat in the egg, whipping cream, and vanilla a extract.

7. Pour this mixture over the pecan pie filling and spread to the edges.

To Bake

8. Wrap the bottom of the springform pan tightly in a large piece of foil. Place a piece of paper towel over the top of the springform pan (not touching the cheesecake) and then wrap foil around the top as well. Your whole pan should be mostly covered in foil to keep out excess moisture.
9. Place the rack that came with your Instant Pot or pressure cooker into the bottom. Pour a cup of water into the bottom.
10. Carefully lower the wrapped cheesecake pan onto the rack (there are ways to do this with a sling made out of tin foil but I didn't bother with that).
11. Close the lid and set the Instant Pot to manual mode for 30 minutes on high. Once the cooking time is complete, let the pressure to release naturally (do not vent it).
12. Lift out the cheesecake and let it cool to room temperature, and then refrigerate for 3 or 4 hours, or even overnight.

Topping

13. In a small saucepan over low heat, melt the butter. Add the sweetener and Yacon syrup and whisk until combined, then stir in the extract and heavy whipping cream.
    Drizzle over the chilled cheesecake and garnish with toasted pecans.

Peanut Butter Mug Cakes

Calories: 210
Fat: 20 g
Carbohydrates: 6 g
Protein: 7 g

Cook Time: 2 minutes
Servings: 6

Ingredients

- 1/3 cup peanut butter
- 1/4 cup butter
- 2/3 cup almond flour
- 1/3 cup Swerve Sweetener
- 2 tsp baking powder
- 2 large eggs
- 1/2 tsp vanilla extract
- 1/4 cup water
- 3 TBSP sugar-free chocolate chips

Instructions

1. In a microwave-safe bowl, melt peanut butter and butter together until smooth.
2. In a medium bowl, whisk together the almond flour, sweetener, and baking powder. Stir in the eggs, vanilla extract, melted peanut butter mixture and water until well combined. Stir in chocolate chips.
3. Divide among 6 ramekins or mugs and microwave each for 1 minute, until puffed and set. Serve warm.

Kentucky Butter Cake

Calories: 310
Fat: 27 g
Carbohydrates: 6 g
Protein: 7 g

Cook Time: 60 minutes
Servings: 16

Ingredients

Cake

- 2 1/2 cups almond flour
- 1/4 cup coconut flour
- 1/4 cup unflavored whey protein powder
- 1 TBSP baking powder
- 1/2 tsp salt
- 1 cup butter, softened
- 1 cup Swerve Granular
- 5 large eggs room temperature.
- 2 tsp vanilla extract
- 1/2 cup whipping cream
- 1/2 cup water

Butter Glaze

- 5 TBSP butter
- 1/3 cup Swerve Granular
- 2 TBSP water
- 1 tsp vanilla extract

Garnish

- 1 to 2 TBSP Confectioner's Swerve

Instructions
1. Preheat oven to 325°F. Grease a bundt cake pan VERY well and then dust with a few tbsp of almond flour.
2. In a medium bowl, whisk together the almond flour, coconut flour, whey protein, baking powder, and salt.
3. In a large bowl, beat the butter and the sweetener together until light and creamy. Beat in the eggs and vanilla extract. Beat in the almond flour mixture and then beat in the whipping cream and water until well combined.
4. Transfer the batter to the prepared baking pan and smooth the top. Bake 50 to 60 minutes, until golden brown and the cake is firm to the touch. A tester inserted in the center should come out clean.
5. Butter Glaze: In a small saucepan over low heat, melt the butter and sweetener together. Whisk until well combined. Whisk in the water and vanilla extract.
6. While the cake is still warm and in the pan, poke holes all over with a skewer. Pour the glaze over and let cool completely in the pan.
7. Gently loosen the sides with a knife or thin rubber spatula, then flip out onto a serving platter. Dust with powdered sweetener.
8. Serve with lightly sweetened whipped cream and fresh berries.

Chocolate Walnut Torte

Calories: 343
Fat: 31 g
Carbohydrates: 9 g
Protein: 9 g

Cook Time: 30 minutes
Servings: 1

Ingredients

Torte
- 1 1/2 cup walnuts
- 3/4 cup Swerve Sweetener
- 1/4 cup cocoa powder
- 1 tsp espresso powder (optional, enhances chocolate flavor)
- 1/2 tsp baking powder
- 1/4 tsp salt
- 1/2 cup butter
- 4 oz unsweetened chocolate
- 5 large eggs
- 1/2 tsp vanilla extract
- 1/2 cup almond milk

Glaze
- 1/2 cup whipping cream
- 2 1/2 oz sugar-free dark chocolate chopped
- 1/3 cup walnut pieces

Instructions

Torte

1. Preheat oven to 325°F and grease a 9-inch round baking pan. Line the bottom with parchment paper and grease the paper.
2. In a food processor, process walnuts until finely ground. Add sweetener, cocoa powder, espresso powder, baking powder, and salt and pulse a few times to combine.
3. In a large saucepan set over low heat, melt butter and chocolate together until smooth. Remove from heat and whisk in eggs and vanilla extract. Add almond milk and whisk until mixture smooths out. Stir in walnut mixture until well combined.
4. Spread batter in prepared baking pan and bake about 30 minutes, until edges are set but center still looks slightly wet. Let cool 15 minutes in pan, then invert onto a wire rack to cool completely. Remove parchment paper.

Glaze

5. In a small saucepan over medium heat, bring cream to just a simmer. Remove from heat and add chopped chocolate. Let sit to melt 5 minutes, then whisk until smooth.
6. Cool another 10 minutes, then pour the glaze over the cake, smoothing the sides. Sprinkle top with walnut pieces and chill until chocolate is firm, about 30 minutes.

Cinnamon Roll Coffee Cake

Calories: 222
Fat: 20 g
Carbohydrates: 5 g
Protein: 7 g

Cook Time: 30 minutes
Servings: 1

Ingredients

Cinnamon Filling

- 3 TBSP Swerve Sweetener
- 2 tsp ground cinnamon

Cake

- 3 cups almond flour
- 3/4 cup Swerve Sweetener
- 1/4 cup unflavored whey protein powder
- 2 tsp baking powder
- 1/2 tsp salt
- 3 large eggs
- 1/2 cup butter, melted
- 1/2 tsp vanilla extract
- 1/2 cup almond milk
- 1 TBSP melted butter

Cream Cheese Frosting

- 3 TBSP cream cheese, softened
- 2 TBSP powdered Swerve Sweetener
- 1 TBSP heavy whipping cream
- 1/2 tsp vanilla extract

Instructions

1. Preheat oven to 325°F and grease an 8x8 inch baking pan.
2. For the filling, combine the Swerve and cinnamon in a small bowl and mix well. Set aside.
3. For the cake, whisk together almond flour, sweetener, protein powder, baking powder, and salt in a medium bowl.
4. Stir in the eggs, melted butter and vanilla extract. Add the almond milk and continue to stir until well combined.
5. Spread half of the batter in the prepared pan, then sprinkle with about two thirds of the cinnamon filling mixture. Spread the remaining batter over top and smooth with a knife or an offset spatula.
6. Bake 35 minutes, or until top is golden brown and a tester inserted in the center comes out with a few crumbs attached.
7. Brush with melted butter and sprinkle with remaining cinnamon filling mixture. Let cool in pan.
8. For the frosting, beat cream cheese, powdered erythritol, cream and vanilla extract together in a small bowl until smooth. Pipe or drizzle over cooled cake.

Gooey Butter Cake

Calories: 269
Fat: 24 g
Carbohydrates: 5 g
Protein: 6 g

Cook Time: 40 minutes
Servings: 15

Ingredients

Cake

- 2 cups almond flour
- 1/2 cup Swerve Sweetener
- 2 TBSP unflavored whey protein powder
- 2 tsp baking powder
- 1/4 tsp salt
- 1/2 cup butter, melted
- 1 large egg
- 1/2 tsp vanilla extract

Filling

- 8 oz cream cheese, softened
- 1/2 cup butter, softened
- 3/4 cup powdered Swerve
- 2 large eggs
- 1/2 tsp vanilla extract
- Powdered Swerve for dusting

Instructions

1. Preheat the oven to 325°F and lightly grease a 9x13 baking pan.
2. In a large bowl, combine the almond flour, sweetener, protein powder, baking powder, and salt. Add the butter, egg, and vanilla extract and stir to combine well. Press into the bottom and partway up the sides of the prepared baking pan.
3. In another large bowl, beat the cream cheese and butter together until smooth. Beat in the sweetener until well combined, then beat in the eggs and vanilla until smooth.
4. Pour the filling over the crust. Bake 35 to 45 minutes, until the filling is mostly set, but the center still jiggles, and the edges are just golden-brown.
5. Remove and let cool, then dust with powdered Swerve and cut into bars.

Classic New York Keto Cheesecake

Calories: 284
Fat: 24 g
Carbohydrates: 3 g
Protein: 5 g

Cook Time: 1 Hour 30 minutes
Servings: 12

Ingredients

- 24 oz cream cheese, softened
- 5 TBSP unsalted butter, softened
- 1 cup powdered Swerve Sweetener
- 3 large eggs, room temperature
- 3/4 cup sour cream, room temperature
- 2 tsp grated lemon zest
- 1 1/2 tsp vanilla extract

Instructions

1. Preheat the oven to 300°F and generously grease a 9-inch springform pan. Cut a circle of parchment to fit the bottom the pan and grease the paper. Wrap 2 pieces of aluminum foil around the outside of the pan to cover the bottom and most of the way up the sides.
2. In a large bowl, beat the cream cheese and butter until smooth, then beat in the sweetener until well combined. Add the eggs, once at a time, beating after each addition. Clean the beaters and scrape down the sides of the bowl as needed.
3. Add the sour cream, lemon zest, and vanilla extract and beat until the batter is smooth and well combined. Pour into the prepared springform pan and smooth the top.

4. Set the pan inside a roasting pan large enough to prevent the sides from touching. Place the roasting pan in the oven and carefully pour boiling water into the roasting pan until it reaches halfway up the sides of the springform pan.
5. Bake 70 to 90 minutes, until the cheesecake is mostly set but still jiggles just a little in the center when shaken. Remove the roasting pan from the one, then carefully remove the springform pan from the water bath. Let cool to room temperature.
6. Run a sharp knife around the edges of the cake to loosen, the release the sides of the pan. Refrigerate for at least 4 hours before serving.

Italian Cream Cake

Calorics: 335
Fat: 30 g
Carbohydrates: 6 g
Protein: 6 g

Cook Time: 45 minutes
Servings: 16

Ingredients

Cake
- 1/2 cup butter, softened
- 1 cup Swerve Sweetener
- 4 large eggs, room temperature, separated
- 1/2 cup heavy cream room temperature
- 1 tsp vanilla extract
- 1 1/2 cups almond flour
- 1/2 cup shredded coconut
- 1/2 cup chopped pecans

- 1/4 cup coconut flour
- 2 tsp baking powder
- 1/2 tsp salt
- 1/4 tsp cream of tartar

Frosting
- 8 oz cream cheese, softened
- 1/2 cup butter, softened
- 1 cup powdered Swerve Sweetener
- 1 tsp vanilla extract
- 1/2 cup heavy whipping cream, room temperature

Garnish
- 2 TBSP shredded coconut, lightly toasted
- 2 TBSP chopped pecans, lightly toasted

Instructions

Cake
1. Preheat the oven to 325°F and grease two 8 inch or 9 inch round cake pans very well (the 8 inch pans will take a little longer to cook but the layers will be higher and I think they will look better). Line the pans with parchment paper and grease the paper.
2. In a large bowl, beat the butter with the sweetener until well combined. Beat in the egg yolks one at a time, mixing well after each addition. Beat in the heavy cream and vanilla extract.
3. In another bowl, whisk together the almond flour, shredded coconut, chopped pecans, coconut flour, baking powder, and salt. Beat into the butter mixture until just combined.
4. In another large bowl, beat the egg whites with the cream of tartar until they hold stiff peaks. Gently fold into the cake batter.
5. Divide the batter evenly among the prepared pans and spread to the edges. Bake 35 to 45 minutes (or longer,

depending on your pans), until the cakes are golden on the edges and firm to the touch in the middle.
6. Remove and let cool completely in the pans, then flip out onto a wire rack to cool completely. Remove the parchment from the layers if it comes out with them.

Frosting
7. In a large bowl, beat the cream cheese and butter together until smooth. Beat in the sweetener and vanilla extract until well combined.
8. Slowly add the heavy whipping cream until a spreadable consistency is achieved.

To Assemble
9. Place the bottom layer on a serving plate and cover the top with about 1/3 of the frosting. Add the next layer and frost the top and the sides.
10. Sprinkle the top with the toasted coconut and pecans. Refrigerate at least half an hour to let set.

Conclusion

I hope you enjoyed our cookbook on "Keto Baking and Keto Dessert Recipes Cookbook: The All in 1 - Low Carb Cookies, Fat Bombs, Low Carb Breads, and Pies.

There are plenty of books on the Keto diet in the market today, so thanks again for choosing this one! Every effort was made to ensure that it is full of as much useful information as possible.

I have tried to keep variety in this book instead of providing a few monotonous recipes like cakes, cookies, etc., so that you can get your hands on various desserts rather than just a few typical ones!

Printed in Great Britain
by Amazon